Beyond Courage

George Cassar

The Canadians at the Second Battle of Ypres

Copyright © 1985 by George Cassar

All rights reserved: no part of this book may be reproduced in any form or by any means, electronic or mechanical, except by a reviewer, who may quote brief passages in a review to be printed in a newspaper or magazine or broadcast on radio or television.

ISBN 0 88750 600 3 (hardcover)
ISBN 0 88750 601 1 (softcover)

Cover painting courtesy Canadian War Museum.
Book design by Michael Macklem.

Printed in Canada

PUBLISHED IN CANADA BY OBERON PRESS

PREFACE

The Second Battle of Ypres will always stand out among the many engagements of the First World War because it was on this occasion that the Germans introduced the horror of poison gas. To Canada the battle has special significance. The men of the 1st Canadian Division were the first soldiers of the Empire to face the new weapon against which they had no defence. For three days these Canadians, in defiance of an almost certain and particularly ugly death, clung heroically to a vital part of the Allied line after the French units on their left had fled in panic. By doing so they saved a quarter of the British forces in France from almost certain destruction. In their first appearance on a European battlefield the Canadians had withstood the test of war. They had proven themselves more than a match for the enemy and not less than the equal of their British comrades in arms. The Second Battle of Ypres gave the Canadians an *esprit de corps* they never lost.

Until now there has not been a single study of the Canadian side of the campaign since the appearance of the Official History in 1938. The interest of this new account may lie in the fact that it is based upon the private papers and personal reminiscences of many of the principal participants, as well as on other documents, which although available to the official historian, was not—or could not—be used by him. The official military historian, Colonel A. Fortescue Duguid, had to work under numerous restrictions and there were many incidents that were treated superficially or omitted altogether. It has now been possible to include much information about which Duguid knew, but which was deemed unsuitable for inclusion in an official history published at a time when most of the leading participants were still alive.

Throughout this work I have made a conscientious attempt to be dispassionate and to bear in mind that, with the advantage of hindsight, even a fool can be wise. It is easy to reflect from the comfort of an easy chair, armed with

5

dispatches, elaborate and accurate diagrams, and descriptions of the battle from both sides, on decisions taken in the midst of terror and confusion. In the heat of battle mistakes are inevitable, often excusable. Having said this I need also add that commanders should be held accountable for errors resulting from ignorance, a false conception of war or want of moral courage.

The account of the Second Battle of Ypres has been written as much for the general reader as for the military student. Technical matters, as a rule, are treated with a minimum of detail and in terms that will be comprehensible to the layman. For the benefit of historians and others interested in the sources from which I drew my material, I have extensively documented the text.

ACKNOWLEDGEMENTS

Many individuals and institutions have contributed to the production of this book. I should like to begin by expressing my indebtedness to my publisher, Dr. Michael Macklem, who encouraged me to write this study and who has been unsparing in his help. Special thanks is also due to Mr. M. Gauvin, Archivist, Public Affairs Section, and Miss Barbara Wilson, Military Specialist, State and Military Records, at the Public Archives, as well as Mr. Paul Marshall, Research Inquirer Assistant, National Defence Headquarters Library in Ottawa. They patiently, diligently and intelligently pursued the many difficult requests that I made of them.

A number of my colleagues at Eastern Michigan University have counselled me in various helpful ways, among them Dr. W.D. Briggs, Lt.-Col. (ret.) Michael Chirio, Dr. Luigi Gimelli, Dr. Richard Goff, Dr. Roger King, Dr. Lester Scherer, Dr. James Waltz, Dr. Ira Wheatley and Dr. Reinhard Wittke. The maps were drawn by Messrs. Thomas Berryman, David Schneider and Donald Ure, under the aegis of Dr. Robert Ward. To all concerned I express my grateful appreciation.

Others whose help was invaluable are Mr. Mac Johnston, Assistant Editor of *Legion Magazine,* Professor Desmond Morton, Erindale College of the University of Toronto, and two survivors of 'Second Ypres,' Captain W.D. Ellis and Sgt.-Maj. A.K. Whyte.

I am grateful to the Canadian Broadcasting Corporation for permission to use excerpts from its interviews with survivors for its radio production 'The Second Battle of Ypres.' In those cases where it has not been possible to trace the holder of the copyright, or where it may have been overlooked, I offer my sincere apologies.

My greatest debt is to my wife, to whom this book is dedicated, for her service as typist as well as for her forebearance and encouragement.

TRAINING THE CEF

The moment Great Britain entered the conflict against Germany on 4 August, 1914, Canada, as part of the empire, was automatically at war. Like the other dominions Canada possessed the right to determine the extent and nature of her participation in the war. There was never any doubt, however, that her contribution would be generous and whole-hearted. During the years immediately before 1914, leaders of the two major political parties had stated unequivocally on a number of occasions that, in the event of a European war, Canada would stand firmly behind Britain. Indeed on 2 August, 1914, two days prior to Britain's declaration of war, the Canadian Prime Minister, Sir Robert Borden, asked London for suggestions as to how Canada could best render effective aid, observing that a considerable force would be available for service abroad.[1] On 6 August the British Government gratefully accepted the Canadian offer of a contingent and the next day requested that it be made up of a division.[2] In Ottawa an Order in Council set the strength of the expeditionary force at 25,000 men.

The most striking feature, given the sharp conflicts that had characterized external affairs in recent years, was the almost complete unanimity with which Canada entered the war. There would be rifts later, when it became apparent that the conflict would not be over and won in short order, but at the outset scarcely a dissenting voice could be heard. At the special session of Parliament, held on 18 August, Wilfred Laurier, Opposition leader, speaking on behalf of his party, accepted the conflict without question, insisting that it was the duty of Canada to support the mother country and to help 'save civilization from the unbridled lust of conquest and power.'[3] In towns and cities across Canada there was much display of patriotic fervour. Crowds gathered to listen to patriotic speeches or surged through the streets singing, cheering and waving flags. All Canadians, from the staunchest Tory to the nationalist of Quebec, appealed for a truce to party and racial disputes and for a vigorous prosecution of the war.[4]

The nation in August 1914 was ill prepared to fight a major war. Canada had a fledgling navy and an air force consisting of two canvas planes still packed in crates. Her Permanent Force was small, a little over 3000 all ranks, and only twelve regular officers had completed staff college courses. Her active militia, although numbering nearly 75,000 men on paper, was far from being a model citizen army. Only about three-quarters of the personnel took part in the brief annual course of training, which consisted mainly of two weeks of foot and rifle drill, field skirmishes, physical exercises and community singing. Many men did not serve out the entire three years of their enlistments and, as the units were always full of raw recruits at each summer camp, training seldom reached beyond the most elementary stages.[5] Moreover they were poorly equipped and inexpertly led by officers and NCOs, nearly all of whom lacked combat experience.

The Dominion Arsenal was equipped to turn out small-arm ammunition and artillery shells but not on the scale to meet the army's war-time needs. It would take many months before Canada could adapt her industries to mass-produce munitions. Until then she would have to compete with the War Office in getting her orders filled from British factories.

An even more desperate situation existed with regard to increasing the stocks of heavy guns. Being dependent on British sources of supply, Canada had some 200 artillery pieces when the war broke out, enough to arm two divisions. Shortly after, however, Ottawa generously contributed 98 field guns to Britain so that when the 2nd Canadian Division was raised there were practically no eighteen-pounders available for its field batteries.[6]

Besides the shortages of ammunition and artillery there were deficiencies in many other vital items of equipment as well as in motor vehicles and horse-drawn transport waggons.

As can be seen Canada did not have in existence anything resembling the expeditionary force she had promised to put in the field. Nevertheless she had the potential to create such a contingent and, if necessary, substantially increase its size. That is, she possessed great quantities of raw materials, well-developed industries, a small but competent professional staff and a large reservoir of men, many of whom were partially trained.

It was the government's wish that the expeditionary force should be composed only of those who volunteered for overseas service. The only question was how to assemble the detachment. A mobilization plan had been prepared in 1911 to raise for service abroad, if need arose, a volunteer force of one division and one cavalry brigade. It provided for a decentralized system and was sufficiently detailed to reduce chaos and confusion to a minimum. The divisional and district commanders were responsible for recruiting and, as far as possible, equipping the men. They were also charged with purchasing horses and waggons from local sources. Enlistment was to be for the duration of the war and preference given to those with military experience or militia training. The troops were to concentrate at Petawawa in summer; in the event mobilization occurred in winter they were to be moved directly to the port of embarkation. The scheme, while not perfect, 'did supply a considered plan for the provision of troops on a fair ratio throughout the Dominion and for a force of the same composition as that called for in August 1914.'[7]

The mobilization plan, carefully prepared by experts against the precise emergency that had now arisen, was consigned to the waste-paper basket by the Minister of Militia, Sam Hughes. A man of great resource and energy, mulish obstinacy and overwhelming vanity, Hughes made his own rules as he went along with the result that many of the things he did had to be undone later on. Why he discarded the prepared scheme is difficult to determine. Some historians feel that it was due to political partisanship, reinforced by his insane egotism. Others attribute his motive to an almost obsessional antipathy toward regular soldiers and regular army methods. Whatever the cause Hughes substituted his own improvised measure, which went into effect on 6 August when he sent 226 night telegrams directly to unit commanders of the militia. With this he short-circuited the whole militia organization, by-passing divisional and district commands while he placed himself in the centre of the mobilization picture. Unit commanders were instructed to interview prospective volunteers between the ages of eighteen and 45 and forward to Ottawa lists of those who could meet the prescribed physical standards. After Militia Headquarters had examined the lists each commander would be told how many to enlist until the required number of men had been obtained.[8]

The selection of 25,000 individuals by this cumbersome system produced instant chaos, from Halifax to Vancouver. Hughes realized the impracticability of the process and on 10 August the duties of the district commander, as envisaged in the 1911 scheme, were restored. Three days later Hughes modified the instructions again. Orders often contradictory and confusing continued to flow from Ottawa but, eventually, most of the volunteers joined through existing militia units in virtually the same manner prescribed by the pre-war mobilization scheme.[9]

In January 1916 the Minister of Militia attempted to justify his actions to Parliament, in terms not only absurd but disingenuous:

> For the first contingent, our recruiting plans were, I think, different from anything that had ever occurred before. There was really a call to arms, like the fiery cross passing through the Highlands of Scotland or the mountains of

Ireland in former days. In place of being forwarded to the district officers commanding, the word was wired to every officer commanding a unit in any part of Canada to buckle on his harness and get busy. The consequence was that in a short time we had the boys on the way for the first contingent, whereas it would have taken several weeks to have got the word around through the ordinary channels.[10]

Hughes is scarcely justified when he asserts that adherence to the original plan would have entailed needless delays. On the contrary, had he used the usual military channels of communication the time required to warn militiamen would have been a matter of hours, not weeks. For example, in 1866 when the Militia Department's organization was much more rudimentary and communications much less developed than in 1914, orders sent through the usual channels twice brought under arms a force of 14,000 Canadian Militia in less than 24 hours. 'It is almost certain,' the militia report of that year went on to say, 'that in place of the ... men called for, 30,000 could have been mustered within 48 hours.'[11] Indeed, because of the confusion caused by Hughes' irregular call to arms, the militia organization quickly regained its normal place in the mobilization scheme.

The call for volunteers met with a ready response. The Western provinces showed the highest percentage of enlistments, partly because the ratio of single men to married men was higher there than elsewhere in Canada. Nearly 65% of all recruits were recent immigrants from Great Britain. In fact in some units there were practically no native-born Canadians.

Most of those who came forward were roused by a sense of duty or adventure. A powerful inducement to enlist in the early days was love of the Empire. There were over one million British-born citizens in Canada, the majority of whom had settled in Ontario and the prairie provinces. They naturally retained strong loyalties to their homeland and the fit men of military age were quick to volunteer for service. Still, there were considerable numbers of Canadians who came forward, indicating how deep-felt was their anxiety to help in the crisis.

It was not the first time that Canada had rendered assistance to the Empire. In 1858, in the midst of the Sepoy rebellion, the 100th Royal Canadian Regiment was dispatched to India; in 1884 a contingent of voyageurs and volunteers served under Wolseley in the Sudan; and about 7300 Canadian troops participated in the South African War. Never before, however, had the very existence of the Empire been at stake. Consequently Canadians answered the call with an enthusiasm that has seldom, if ever, been matched by a former British colony. From the workshops and offices in the cities, lumber and mining camps, vast wheat fields of the prairies, farms and orchards in the east, the manhood of the nation converged upon the recruiting centres in limitless numbers. [12] Within a month the government, which had asked for 20,000 men, found almost twice that number at its disposal and the Militia Department was compelled to issue orders suspending the enrollment of additional recruits. [13]

From local assembly areas the volunteers marched to the rail station where they entrained for Valcartier, sixteen miles northwest of Quebec city. The government had selected the site in 1912 as a central training area for the Quebec militia but when the war broke out it was still a wilderness of wooded and sandy flatlands. The official reason for building a new camp at Valcartier, rather than using the facilities at Petawawa, was that its proximity to the embarkation port of Quebec city would reduce transportation costs.

Under the supervision of Sam Hughes, ably assisted by William Price, a timber baron, and James McCarty, a civil engineer, the work of construction began on 8 August. Overnight the new camp site swarmed with construction workers, lumberjacks clearing bush and trees, and contractors hastily delivering horses, waggons, boats, tentage and other para-

14

phernalia of war. Progress was phenomenal. In less than a month the place was transformed into a huge military camp with facilities to accommodate the thousands of recruits. Valcartier stands as a monument to Hughes' unbounded optimism and driving power but as Professor Stanley has correctly observed, it was 'wasteful and unnecessary.'[14]

The first wave of volunteers arrived on 18 August amid construction and confusion, and by 8 September the number of all ranks had reached the maximum of 32,665. Among these was a battalion of ex-soldiers raised by Hamilton Gault, a Montreal businessman, who also contributed $100,000 toward its costs. Named after the beautiful daughter of the Governor General, the Princess Patricia's Canadian Light Infantry was quickly recruited in Ottawa from among former British regulars and Canadian veterans of the South African War.[15] In December the 'Patricias,' as they are commonly called, were the first Canadian troops to land in France.

The authorized strength of the Canadian expeditionary force was 25,000 men, not the more than 32,000 that had been assembled at Valcartier. Six thousand or so of them, after eagerly volunteering for service, faced the bitter prospect of being sent back home. During a visit to Valcartier on 21 September the Prime Minister, having concluded that the 1st Division would require reinforcements and reserves once it reached the front, decided to send the entire force. Hughes, who had agonized over the choice of who should go and who should remain, 'broke down and sobbed' in relief.[16]

On 1 September, after some reshuffling, the infantry was organized into four brigades, each comprising four battalions of 1000 men. The 1st Brigade, made up of the 1st, 2nd, 3rd and 4th Battalions from Ontario, was commanded by Lt.-Col. M.S. Mercer. The 2nd Brigade under Lt.-Col. A.W. Currie consisted of the 5th, 6th, 7th and 8th Battalions, all from the west. Colonel R.E.W. Turner's 3rd Brigade was composed of one battalion from Montreal and the maritimes, the 14th, and three Highland battalions from across Canada, the 13th, 15th and 16th. The 4th Brigade, consisting of the 9th, 10th and 11th Battalions from the prairies, and the 12th from the maritimes, was allocated to Lt.-Col. J.E. Cohoe. Another battalion (the 17th) was formed to handle the surplus infantry as a result of a decision on 21 September to send all medically fit volunteers overseas.[17]

The new battalions, designated as they were by numbers only, failed to perpetuate the time-honoured names of militia units.[18] The more than 32,000 men making up the expeditionary force represented some 200 militia organizations across Canada. Naturally each unit wanted to prove its mettle in action under its own name and its own officers. The new system, in addition to creating hard feelings, particularly among units with a long and distinguished record of service, hindered training and retarded the growth of regimental *esprit de corps*.

Of special interest to Hughes in the early weeks of the war was the selection of a commander for the Canadian division. There is not much doubt that the Minister of Militia would have relished the post himself. On 14 August Borden cabled Sir G.H. Perley, the acting Canadian High Commissioner in London, that Hughes would probably go overseas 'if convinced that he would command Canadian division ... and be in fighting line.'[19] Although a colonel in the militia, Hughes was by experience and temperament totally unsuited for combat leadership. Lord Kitchener, British Secretary of State for War, settled the issue when he told Perley that it would be a mistake to change the Minister of Militia 'at this juncture.' Thereafter Hughes, having accepted the judgment of the War Office, did not even insist on the appointment of a Canadian. Indeed when Kitchener recommended a choice from three Canadian-born officers serving in the British Army,[20] Hughes considered none of these sufficiently senior or suitable for high command. Instead he had in mind three British officers with whom he was familiar and of these three he thought that Maj.-Gen. E.A.H. Alderson was 'the best qualified by far.'[21] On 5 September Kitchener notified Perley that he was glad to be able to comply with Hughes' wishes.[22] Alderson's appointment was made official on 25 September, and he was promoted to the rank of Lt.-Gen. effective 14 October, the day the first Canadian units arrived in Great Britain.

Now that a commander had been chosen the next step was to resolve the delicate matter of the relation of the Canadian contingent to the British Army. In the past Canadian forces sent to fight overseas had been dispersed among British units. The same procedure might have been followed in 1914 but the Canadian expeditionary force was the outcome of national will and pride and the government was anxious that it should remain a national formation. Kitchener apparently raised no objection. However, there is an account that suggests otherwise.

In late October the Minister of Militia sailed for England to brief Alderson 'respecting officer and other important matters.'[23] While in London Hughes visited the War Office and, according to a Canadian officer who was present, was told that the Canadian regiments were to be broken up and integrated in the British Army.[24] Supposedly Hughes told Kitchener to go to the devil and in the end succeeded in having the order rescinded. The story is probably untrue. The statements of the officer in question were made in June 1934, almost twenty years later, and no evidence can be found either in private or official records to corroborate them. If such an event had occurred Hughes most assuredly would have proclaimed it loudly to the country since he was not in the habit of concealing his accomplishments, especially as a champion of Canadian rights.

Early on, the Militia Department made arrangements for the Canadian force to complete its training on Salisbury Plain in England. Valcartier could not be used as a winter camp and besides Hughes was anxious to get Canadian troops overseas.[25] All the leading military authorities in Europe, with

17

the exception of Lord Kitchener,[26] had predicted that the conflict would last six months or less. The most frequent fear of Canadian soldiers of all ranks was that the great adventure would be over before they could reach the field.

The weather was pleasant enough and the men experienced little hardship at Valcartier, although there were shortages of practically everything in the beginning. The time for training, already limited, was further shortened by interruptions of one kind or another. The recruits, arriving with no unit organization, had to be medically examined, inoculated, attested and issued clothing and equipment, which, in many instances, came belatedly from the manufacturers. There were changes, practically on a daily basis, in the composition, location and command of the units. To make matters worse there was the omnipresence of Sam Hughes. He loved to take the salute at full-dress parades, exercised close control in matters of administration and training and made appointments in a seigniorial manner without reference to the militia council or to his colleagues. All of this had a disruptive effect on the men's training program.

The basic principles, as regards training, were contained in a manual entitled *Memorandum for Camps of Instruction, 1914*. The first few days were devoted to elementary squad and foot drill and rifle instruction. Then came route marches of increasing length, together with daily physical exercises, necessary for the hardening process. Units, with experienced and resourceful officers as well as a large portion of militia-trained personnel, progressed rapidly and even conducted night manoeuvres.

After six weeks the Canadian expeditionary force, still relatively disorganized and untrained, prepared to leave for England. The contingent of nearly 33,000 men consisted of seventeen infantry battalions, in addition to the Patricias, three field artillery brigades and three regular formations— the Royal Canadian Horse Artillery, the Royal Canadian Dragoons and Lord Strathcona's Horse. Initially plans for the

Canadian division had not included any units of the Permanent Force, an organization that Hughes had never regarded with particular favour. But, as so often happened with the erratic Hughes, orders changed and in the end it was decided to send one artillery brigade and two cavalry regiments.[27] The Royal Canadian Regiment, the only regular infantry battalion of the Permanent Force, was sent to Bermuda to relieve a British regiment in garrison for service in France.[28]

The embarkation of the force began on 23 September. William Price, the man who had performed such prodigious feats of construction at Valcartier, was appointed to supervise the embarkation. He was not provided with a staff to assist him and his own efforts to obtain experienced officers from Valcartier proved unsuccessful. With no plan to follow Price had to improvise as he went along and it is not surprising, to use the words of a high-ranking official, that 'chaos reigned supreme.'[29] Many units were split up and separated from their equipment; stores were left behind; and some ships were grossly overloaded while others were half empty.

On the last day of September the transport ships, one by one, began to move out into the St. Lawrence, on their way to rendezvous with escorting British ships in Gaspé Harbour. Here Sam Hughes, in a rented tugboat, passed through the convoy distributing printed copies of his farewell speech to the troops. On one of the convoys there were tense moments when the Minister's launch was seen approaching. The men were lined up for their ration of beer, which had been provided by a kindly benefactor from Quebec City. A ministerial order, however, had prohibited the consumption of alcoholic beverages on board ship. The captain was spared embarrassment and possible disciplinary action when Hughes' launch veered off at the last moment.

At 3 PM on 3 October, in clear weather, the flotilla sailed. The 32 ships, strung out over 21 miles, took three hours to stream through the harbour's narrow exit into the Gulf of St.

Lawrence. Once out at sea the ships moved into three lines, two miles apart, each led by a British cruiser with a fourth cruiser lying well back astern. The Canadian division was the largest armed force ever to cross the Atlantic. No-one knew at the time that it was only the vanguard of a much larger host.

The crossing was uneventful although on the last day reports of German submarines in the English Channel caused the convoy to change its destination from Southampton to Plymouth. The leading transports entered Plymouth Sound on 14 October and, as the other ships arrived, the port became congested, delaying the landing of some units until the 24th. The townspeople, kept in the dark until the last moment, lined the waterfront and wharves, shouting 'bravo Canadians' and greeting the disembarking troops with cheers, handshakes and kisses. A Canadian officer (Major A.J.E. Kirkpatrick) wrote: 'We are the first troops to arrive from the overseas Dominions and the papers say so many kind things of Canada and of us that we will have difficulty in living up to the high standards they are setting us.'[30]

Among the many dignitaries on hand was General Alderson, commander of the Canadian force. Born in 1859, Alderson had seen much active service in Egypt, the Sudan and South Africa during his 36 years of army experience. His first association with Canadian troops was in 1900, when the Royal Canadian Dragoons and 2nd Canadian Rifles had formed part of his Mounted Infantry Column for seven months—a decisive factor in his present appointment. His war record had earned him, in addition to mentions in a number of dispatches, numerous decorations, among them the Khedive's Bronze Star, the Queen's Medal with five clasps and the King's Medal with two clasps. A great source of pride to him was the bronze medal of the Royal Humane Society, awarded for rescuing a private soldier from the turbulent waters of the Nile.[31] Short, dark with a bushy moustache, he was highly respected for his soldierly qualities and kind, gentle character.

LIEUTENANT-GENERAL E.A.H. ALDERSON

From Plymouth the Canadian force faced a seven-hour train journey, followed by a march of eight or ten miles, before reaching the wilds of Salisbury Plain. Purchased by the War Office in 1900 the camp site, approximately twelve miles long and six miles wide, had been used as a military training ground for the Regular Army and Territorial Forces. The Canadians were assigned to four main areas extending along a five-mile strip on the western side. There were no permanent barracks available for them but, while the convoy was crossing the Atlantic, fatigue parties from the Territorial Force, assisted by a group of New Zealanders who had recently enlisted in England, had set up thousands of bell tents, marquees and kitchen shelters.

The last Canadian units had not yet arrived in camp when the fine autumn weather broke. A heavy downpour brought a quarter of an inch of rain on 21 October and a full inch in the next five days. It was the start of what would turn out to be the worst winter in recent memory. Rain fell on 89 of the 123 days between the middle of October 1914 to the middle of February 1915. The 29.3 inches of precipitation for that period almost doubled the average for the preceding 32 years.

Conditions in the camp grew progressively worse. A layer of chalk several inches below ground level prevented drainage. The turf cut by marching men, horses' hoofs and waggon wheels turned into a quagmire. The tents were not waterproof and the poor quality of the canvas merely broke the heavier drops into fine particles of spray that settled and drenched everything within. On 11 November, and again a month later, storms reaching gale proportions levelled many tents, leaving the occupants shivering and wet, scattering correspondence and articles over the muddy field. Major Kirkpatrick has provided us with a graphic account of his tribulations during one such stormy day:

Pouring rain again. After parade, I changed my wet clothes in a very wet tent, snatching my dry things out of

22

my tin box, with water dropping all the time. Books, papers and everything uncovered are wet through. At 5 PM walked down to 2nd Battalion mess tent to a lecture. Pitch dark, black as a hat and blowing a gale. Fell over a tent guy and took a roll in the mud. Lecture inaudible on account of the roaring of the wind and the rain on the tent. Suddenly at 5.30 with a report like a shot, snap went the guy ropes, crack went the pole and down on our heads came the soaking canvas, chasing us all out into the driving rain, now turned to sleet. So cold and pitiless was the wind one could hardly stand up. Nearly all the large tents went down ... I found myself up to my knees in mud in the wild blackness searching for the road, then struggled back, joyful to find the men's tents standing and mine also. But the rain, driven by that wind, went clean through our rotten tents, soaked everything inside and gave us a very miserable night.[32]

Training was resumed during the first week of November. All instructors were members of the Canadian contingent except for two officers and five NCOs loaned by the War Office. The time for basic infantry training was devoted chiefly to physical conditioning, foot and arms drill, musketry practice and entrenching. This was followed by five weeks of company training, two weeks of battalion training and a similar period of brigade training. Target practice was stressed in the training schedule. Each infantryman shot off his allotted 155 rounds and for about ten minutes a day practised charger-loading and rapid-fire with dummy cartridges. The idea was to attain a standard comparable to that of the British Regular divisions in France, which had amazed the enemy with the speed and accuracy of their rifle fire.

The miserable weather played havoc with the training schedule. Cold conditions or mist hampered range practice; heavy storms of wind and rain interrupted tactical exercises. Men had to plough through ankle-deep mud all day, their clothing soaked by rain or caked with slime. Much of the time little or nothing was done. Indeed one unit historian records that out of a total of 130 days spent in England only 40 were available for training.[33] According to Colonel Duguid, few of those who served on the Western front in the next four years were called upon to suffer such prolonged and unavailing misery as was endured on Salisbury Plain in the winter of 1914. As a matter of fact it was because of the experiences of the Canadians on the Plain that the Canberra government ordered the Australians and New Zealanders to disembark in Egypt, instead of proceeding to England.[34]

It is remarkable, in view of the prevailing conditions, that the soldiers, whatever their innermost thoughts, generally remained uncomplaining. The same feeling that had existed at Valcartier, that is, that they might not be ready to play a role in the imminent rout of the German Army, spurred them on, enabling them to withstand all hardships and overcome all difficulties. The Canadian High Command naturally worried lest the prolonged period of inclement weather affect the level of morale. On the last day of November, after a brutal stretch of rain and sleet, General Alderson visited camp and talked to some of the officers. He asked if the men were complaining about the field conditions. On receiving a negative answer, he remarked, 'Wonderful! Simply wonderful!'[35]

The let-down that the military leaders feared never occurred. Early in January 1915 weather conditions improved and there was a noticeable change in the attitude of the men even though training was intensified. The haggard and painful look on their faces disappeared, they joked and engaged in horseplay during idle moments and even their most blasphemous comments on the weather and mud were salted with good humour. On route marches they sang and, as with British troops, by far their favourite tune was the lifting 'Tipperary,' a pre-war music-hall hit.

The time in England was spent not only to train but also to

reorganize battalions and exchange defective equipment. At Valcartier there had been eight companies per battalion. In November the War Office decreed that the battalions, in accordance with British establishment, should reorganize on a four-company basis. In the next two months the War Office changed its mind half a dozen times until finally adopting the four-company system.

A good deal of effort and expense had gone into equipping the Canadian division. Many of the items issued back in Canada did not conform to British pattern and, after careful scrutiny, some were ordered replaced. Of immediate concern were the men's boots. Each recruit was supplied with a single pair of boots from a model found satisfactory by Canadians in the South African war and that had become standard issue for the Permanent Force ever since. The Canadian boots were not designed for heavy marching and continual soaking in mud. An emergency shipment of 48,000 pairs of overshoes arrived from Canada in November but these were of little help. On Alderson's recommendation each soldier was issued a pair of the sturdier British regulation boots.

The Division had only five battalions that brought web equipment from Canada. The remainder wore the obsolescent Oliver pattern that had pouches for 80 rounds of ammunition instead of 150, no pack facilities for carrying entrenchment tools and pinched and chafed wearers under the arms. Drawing upon War Office stock Alderson issued web equipment to seven Canadian battalions.

Similarly the Mac Adam shovel, intended for use as a shield and as an entrenching tool, proved unsuitable for service in the field. Hughes had taken a special interest in this device that was patented by and named after his secretary, Ena Mac Adam. When stuck into the ground in front of a prone rifleman, it was supposed to serve as a bullet-proof shield. The steel blade was eight-and-a-half by nine-and-three-quarters inches with a thickness of three-sixteenths of an inch and in the centre were two holes, one to shoot and a smaller one to sight through.[36] The tests showed that the shovels were useless for either purpose. Quite apart from the fact that that they were 'heavy and difficult to carry, chafed the thighs and banged about,' they were awkward to dig with and could not stop a bullet. They were replaced by British equipment and eventually sold as scrap metal.

Unfortunately the most important item used by the soldier was not exchanged. The Canadians were armed with the Ross rifle, which was longer, heavier and less reliable than the British Lee-Enfield. In 1902 the Canadian government, after fruitless efforts during previous years to place orders in England for the supply of rifles for its military forces, adopted the Ross rifle and entered into a contract with the inventor, Sir Charles Ross. Misfortune plagued the Ross from the outset. Faults of varying seriousness caused so many modifications that by the time the war broke out the original Ross had been altered almost beyond recognition. In both the press and parliament the relative merits of the Ross was a subject of widespread controversy. When the Conservatives defeated the Liberals in 1911, after wandering in the wilderness of opposition for 15 years, Sam Hughes became an ardent and active champion of the Ross. His efforts at silencing the critics were strengthened by the stunning successes gained by Canadian marksmen using the Ross at Bisley (1911 and 1913) and other target ranges.

The failings of the Ross, about which critics had warned, surfaced again at Valcartier, and later on at Salisbury. Experienced soldiers freely admitted that the Ross, under the orderly conditions of the target range, was a superior rifle. On the other hand they were equally convinced that it was unsuited for the harsh exigencies of field service. They observed that back sights were frequently damaged by catching on equipment or broken during bayonet instruction; that there were many weak striker and magazine springs; and more significantly that the rifle jammed and misfired under rapid fire. The many complaints reaching Alderson's office

26

were forwarded to Ottawa, which refused to withdraw the rifle. Hughes insisted that with further modifications the Ross would meet his earlier claim of being the 'most perfect military rifle in every sense in the World today.'[37] Thus to satisfy one man's insane ego the men in the ranks were doomed to carry into battle an inferior rifle with predictable calamitous results.

The general health of the troops was surprisingly good given their continued exposure to the wretched weather. The number of sick did increase, however, after the 2nd, 3rd and 4th brigades moved into permanent accommodations. The building of huts on the Plain had begun early in October but at Christmas time 11,000 Canadians were still under canvas —indeed the 1st brigade remained in tents until departing for France. The huts were intended to accommodate 30 men but they were invariably overcrowded. The proximity of the men to one another, together with improper sanitary precautions, resulted in outbreaks of various contagious diseases, in particular meningitis with 28 cases proving fatal.

Posing a greater worry to Canadian Headquarters than the question of sickness was the widespread ill discipline among the rank and file. A large portion of the contingent consisted of raw recruits who were independent-minded, hardy with a devil-may-care attitude. They dressed sloppily, did not snap to attention like the British soldier when the national anthem was played, frequently called their superiors by their first name and if they saluted their officers at all did so in the most casual and indifferent manner. Few men seemed to be concerned that a pass was required before leaving camp; and those that obtained formal leave, more often than not, created disturbances in the neighbouring towns or returned late and drunk. 'We must not expect Canadians,' one newspaper warned the angry local citizens, 'to behave as our men do. Anglo-Saxon though they are, they come to us from a rude frontier country where class and rank are unimportant.'

Undoubtedly the existing conditions on Salisbury Plain

exacerbated the troops' tendency for mischief. Generally the offences were not serious but inconsequential and harmless; most could have been stopped with a simple warning. However, the newly appointed officers and NCOs had not developed the talent to manage men and they frequently created hard feelings by employing bullying tactics or imposing punishments that exceeded the nature of the infractions.

Alderson personally took the matter in hand and announced near the end of October that he would establish wet canteens in the camp, at which beer might be sold at certain hours and under careful supervision. This, he was convinced, would reduce the men's visit to nearby villages where 'they get bad liquor, become quarrelsome and then create disturbances.'[38] Despite protests from temperance groups in Canada the new arrangements were put into effect. 'The wet canteens,' an officer commented, 'is a Godsend and drinking has been reduced to a minimum. A man who is free to buy a mug of beer a couple of times a day does not try to keep a bottle of whisky in his tent.'[39] An additional measure entitled a deserving soldier to a six-day pass with a free ticket to anywhere in the British Isles. At the same time those in charge of discipline came to understand that a blend of firmness and subtle cajolery would cause men to conform willingly.[40] All of this produced the desired results. Morale improved while drunkenness dwindled and offences of all sorts decreased.

In mid November the Patricias, the most experienced battalion, moved to Winchester to join the 80th Brigade, which formed part of the 27th (British) Division. On 21 December, re-equipped with the Lee-Enfield rifle, they sailed for France.[41]

Six weeks later the 1st Division was ready. On 4 February, 1915, the Division was paraded at Knighton Down for an inspection by His Majesty the King, a sure sign of impending departure. The Canadian contingent, drawn up in two lines at 200 paces distance, gave the royal salute when His Majesty stepped out of his coach and onto the platform.

There was a cold stiff breeze and a heavy downpour as the King, accompanied by Lord Kitchener, walked down the entire line, almost two miles long, shaking hands with each commander and wishing him and his regiment 'good luck.' The King was in good spirits and looked healthy and, once he returned to the stand, the division marched past in double lines. The troops then lined the railway four deep and, with hats aloft on bayonets, 'cheered like mad' as His Majesty stood at the window of the royal coach and waved farewell.[42]

In six months Canada had mobilized, assembled a division out of the civilian sector, equipped it and partially trained it; then sent it off to England where some of its equipment was replaced and its training and organization completed. It was an incredible accomplishment. Indeed the actual training time allotted to the Canadian force was less than British military analysts had calculated would be required to put their own Territorial divisions in the field. The Territorials, like the Canadian militia, had some training but the first division did not arrive in France until 24 February, 1915. On the other hand Kitchener's New Armies (British divisions raised from volunteers at the outbreak of war) began the crossing only during the second week in May.

The units of the Canadian division began to leave Salisbury on 7 February, boarding trains that proceeded to take them to Avonmouth on the Bristol Channel. The first to make the crossing were fortunate. The later groups, crowded below decks in the cold dark holds of small cargo boats, experienced the most disagreeable journey. A westerly gale and turbulent seas pitched and rolled the ships, causing severe sea sickness to all but a few on board. To add to the unpleasantness, cold waves broke over the deck and drenched the men huddled in the holds.[1] Normally a 36-hour passage there were so many tedious delays at either end of the journey that some men were forced to remain on board for five days. Yet practically all bore their adversity with admirable patience, no doubt relieved at leaving the misery of Salisbury Plain.

The ships docked at the port of St. Nazaire and, as a strike of stevedores was in progress, the unloading was done by work parties furnished by the units themselves. Generally the men arrived well equipped to deal with the raw, cold French winter but if not they were issued such items as they required.[2] Many soldiers supplemented their two days' rations of bully beef and hardtack by buying a loaf of bread (*baguette*), which they carried under the straps of their packs. The Canadians, like the British troops that preceded them to France, were admonished to behave themselves. Pasted in each man's pay book was a printed message from Lord Kitchener:

Be invariably courteous, considerate and kind. Never do anything likely to injure or destroy property, and always look upon looting as a disgraceful act. You are sure to meet with a welcome and to be trusted; your conduct must justify that welcome and trust. Your duty cannot be done unless your health is sound. So keep constantly on your guard against any excesses. In this new experience you may find temptations both in wine and women. You must entirely resist both temptations, and, while treating all women with perfect courtesy, you should avoid any intimacy.[3]

The arrival of a Canadian contingent on French soil was a historic occasion. There were messages of welcome from the mayor and other officials of St. Nazaire. The townspeople lined the streets, becoming doubly excited on hearing their native language spoken by Canadians of French descent. Along the way the Canadians were supplied with refreshments and showered with blessings, good wishes and shouts of *'vive le Canada.'* At the railway station the troops were crammed into dirty little freight cars marked *'Hommes 40, Chevaux 8'* (meaning 40 men to a car or, alternatively, eight horses) and carried 400 miles north-east to their billeting area near Hazebrouck. Here on 20 February they were inspected by Sir John French, the British Commander-in-Chief. 'They appear to be a fine lot of men,' French wrote in his diary, 'and I like the look of the Division.'[4]

The Canadians were about to enter a conflict that had become deadlocked after the initial exertions of the belligerents. In August 1914 both sides had relied on long standing plans to gain a quick offensive victory. The German Schlieffen Plan called for a holding operation on the left while the strong right wing wheeled through Belgium, captured Paris and then fell on the rear of the French armies.[5] With the French beaten, German trains would rush the victorious troops to the eastern front to augment the small force that had been assigned to hold off the slow-moving Russians. The French, in accordance with Plan XVII, aimed to launch a violent offensive into Alsace and Lorraine.[6] They confidently assumed that their offensive would compel the Germans to abandon their outflanking movement. Ironically it worked the other way. After a month of fighting the Germans were almost within sight of Paris but the French were in retreat everywhere.[7]

As the campaign in northern France approached its climax the German supreme commander, Helmuth von Moltke, made a costly miscalculation. He changed the direction of the extreme right wing army, sending it to the east, rather than to the west, of Paris. His intention was to close the gap that had formed between the extreme right and the other armies taking part in the offensive. The French saw that the Germans, instead of executing a dreaded flanking movement, had exposed their own flank. General Joffre, the French army chief, was persuaded to hurl every available man against the German flank and rear. On 6 September Joffre, having regrouped his forces and with strong support from the relatively small British contingent, launched a general counter-offensive along the Marne River. After four days of bitter fighting the Germans stopped their advance and withdrew. The battle of the Marne wrecked Germany's hope for a quick victory over France and forced her into the protracted two-front war she had so desperately sought to avoid.

The Germans fell back across the Aisne River to a previously prepared position. There they held, despite repeated Allied attacks. After the battle line hardened behind the Aisne both sides attempted to out flank each other in what popularly became known as the 'race to the sea.' As each effort failed the line moved farther and farther north until it reached the sea. At the close of 1914 the belligerents faced each other in two solid lines of trenches that stretched nearly 500 miles, from the Channel coast to Switzerland. The war of movement now settled into a war of position.

Throughout the winter of 1914-1915 the opposing armies built elaborate trench systems complete with concrete emplacements, underground shelters and machine-gun nests and protected by thick entanglements of barbed wire. Behind the front line were other lines to which soldiers could retreat and from which support could be sent. In between the hostile trenches lay 'no man's land,' a strip of desolation filled with

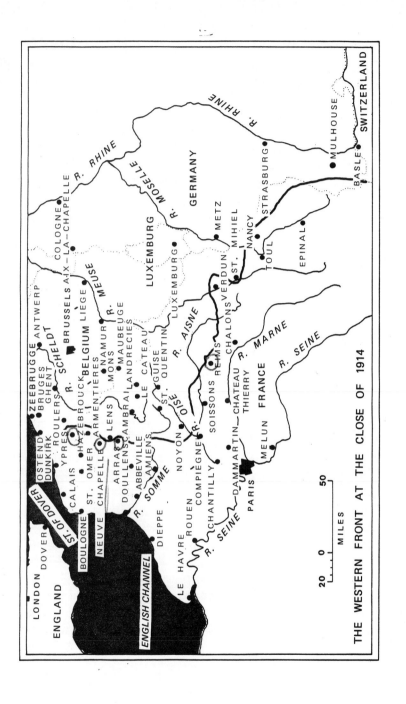

THE WESTERN FRONT AT THE CLOSE OF 1914

shell holes, tree stumps and the general debris of constant fighting.

Since flanking movements were no longer possible the enemy had to be assaulted frontly, that is, in the most difficult and costly manner. In such warfare artillery, heavy and light, took on increased importance. Initially the conventional plan for a break-through called for a preliminary bombardment that was intended to break up the barbed wire, silence the machine-guns and leave the occupants in the trenches dazed and demoralized. Then, as the artillery ceased, the infantry would climb over the top of the parapets in waves, and with fixed bayonets, rush toward the enemy lines. All too often it was discovered that the barrage had not done what it was expected to do with the result that the machine-gunners were able to get back into position and mercilessly strafe the advancing columns. If the assulting troops did penetrate the front trenches of the enemy they would soon be thrown back by a counter-attack. As a result gains were minimal and losses tremendous.

For much of 1915 the Germans remained on the defensive in the west, concentrating on trying to knock-out the Russians. The initiative therefore passed to the French and the British. The French, because of their preponderant military strength, dominated the alliance. Their strategy was governed by the idea of liberating northern France by means of frontal assaults. Thus the Anglo-French armies were in the unenviable position of having lost ground during mobile warfare and then committed to retaking it under conditions that gave every advantage to the defenders.

The line that took shape after the first four months of fighting would not change appreciably until 1918. In the north the Belgian Army was entrenched between two French detachments, one at Nieuport and the other in the vicinity of Ypres. Below Ypres the British defended the line as far south as Givenchy. French forces held the remainder of the front to the Swiss border. Commanding the French divisions in the north, from Arras to the sea, was General Ferdinand Foch whose headquarters were at Cassel. As Joffre's deputy he was also charged with co-ordinating the operations of his armies with those of the British and Belgians.

By the end of 1914 British commitment to the Western front had grown from six to sixteen divisions (eleven infantry and five cavalry). This enabled Sir John French to divide his forces into two armies. The First Army under General Douglas Haig occupied an eleven-mile line between Bois Grenier and Givenchy. On its left was General Horace Smith-Dorrien's Second Army, which carried the front for seventeen miles to Ypres.[8] The Canadian contingent was assigned initially to the First Army and later to the Second.

Before the Canadians participated in active operations they were given a brief introduction into the intricacies of trench warfare. After leaving their billeting area they were attached for a week to British units holding the line in front of Armentières. Each soldier, from Company commander down to private, spent 48 hours with a corresponding member of the host unit for individual instruction. That was followed by 24 hours of platoon training during which each Canadian platoon assumed responsibility for a definite length of trench line. The indoctrination here was far different from anything the Canadians had experienced at Valcartier and Salisbury but all ranks accommodated themselves quickly to the new outlook and readily assimilated the proferred information. Pronounced ready the 1st Canadian Division received orders to take over 6400 yards of line south of Armentières (Fleurbaix sector). Alderson visited many of the units before they entered the line for the first time. He cautioned the men to refrain from exposing themselves unnecessarily, to avoid shooting at nonexistent targets and to 'sit low and sit tight' during the bombardment 'for there is nothing else to do.' He observed that if there was one thing the Germans could not stand it was a bayonet attack. He encouraged the Canadians to use the bayonet whenever practical, confident that they had the strength to drive it home. He ended by saying:

> My old regiment, the Royal West Kent, has been here
> since the beginning of the war and it has never lost a
> trench. The Army says, 'The West Kents never budge.' I
> am proud of the great record of my old Regiment. And I
> think it is a good omen. I now belong to you and you
> belong to me: and before long the Army will say: 'The
> Canadians never budge.' Lads it can be left there, and there
> I leave it. The Germans will never turn you out.[9]

Between the 1st and 3rd of March the Canadians—eager,
doubtful, anxious—reached their assigned place in the line.
The Canadian front was divided into three sections, each of
which was held by one infantry brigade with an affiliated field
artillery brigade. There were now only three infantry
brigades—the 1st, 2nd and 3rd. The 4th disappeared as a formation after Alderson decreed on 18 January that its battalions, along with the 17th Battalion, would supply reinforcements for the other brigades.[10]

Each brigade had two battalions at one time in the front
line, the remainder being kept in the rear. Each battalion
spent four successive days on duty at the front. At the end of
the fourth day the battalion was replaced by a fresh one and
went back to rest in billets.

The three infantry brigade commanders had each a long
and distinguished record of service in the militia. All were
promoted to brigadier-general. M.S. Mercer was 55 years old
and in private life was a successful lawyer. He gained his commission in the 2nd Regiment (Queen's Own Rifles of Canada)
in Toronto in 1885 and rose to command that unit 26 years
later. He was adjutant of the Canadian Bisley team in 1909
and more significant had graduated from the Militia Staff
Course. Keen, personally fearless with a firm grasp of detail
and a real capacity for administration, his tragic death in
1916[11] deprived the army of one of its ablest and most

BRIGADIER-GENERAL M.S. MERCER

promising leaders.

Born in 1875 outside the tiny Ontario village of Strathroy, A.W. Currie[12] grew up on his father's farm and studied to become a school teacher. At nineteen he left home to live in British Columbia where he taught school for five-and-a-half years before selling insurance and speculating on an increasing scale in real estate. He began his military career in 1897 by joining the 5th Regiment of the BC Brigade, Canadian Garrison Artillery, as a gunner. Commissioned in 1900 he passed through the ranks until he was gazetted to command the regiment. During the time he was in charge of the 5th Regiment it attained a very high standard of efficiency, winning in 1912 and 1913 all the first and second places in artillery competition conducted under the auspices of the Dominion Artillery Association. In January 1914 he assumed command of the newly formed 50th Regiment, Gordon Highlanders of Canada and several months later passed the Militia Staff Course. His financial plight had deterred him from volunteering for active service on the outbreak of war but, upon being approached by Hughes, accepted the offer to command a brigade.

Currie had little training by professional standards. Nor did he cut a very soldierly figure. Over six feet tall and bulky with a jowled face, sizeable paunch and a seat of generous proportions, he resembled one of the first lumbering tanks. Nevertheless he had a flair for military command. An intelligent, thoughtful person, free of military ideas conceived and employed over the past century, he brought to his task a fresh eye and an open mind. Within a few years he would emerge as one of the outstanding officers of his day. Indeed it is almost certain that if Lloyd George had decided to replace Haig as commander of the British forces in France Currie would have been one of the leading candidates for the appointment.

R.E.W. Turner was 43, a short bespectacled man who looked as if he might feel more at home in the office of his wholesale firm than on the battlefield. Gazetted 2nd Lieu-

LIEUTENANT-GENERAL SIR ARTHUR CURRIE, GCMG, KCB

tenant in the 10th Queen's Own Canadian Hussars in 1892, he had served in South Africa with the Royal Canadian Dragoons. He was awarded the Victoria Cross in 1900 for his part in a rearguard action at Leliefontein in which two Canadian field guns were saved from capture and a British column from encirclement. On returning to civilian life Turner remained in the militia and was placed on the Reserve of Officers in 1912. While no-one could doubt his courage, energy and zeal he was without other qualities vital in a front-line commander. In particular he lacked decisiveness and a thorough grasp of his profession and it was said after the war that he was like putty in the hands of his brigade-major, Garnet Hughes (son of the Minister of Militia).

More than two-thirds of the officers in the expeditionary force were Canadian-born and practically all of them had been trained in the militia. The British provided the rest of the officers, especially for senior general staff positions—it must be remembered that up to 1914 few Canadians had passed through the Staff College at Camberley. The British officers selected to serve in the Canadian Division were soldiers of high quality. They included many who would advance far in their profession.

The Canadian sector in front of Fleurbaix was quiet, except for occasional shells screaming by or snipers' bullets zipping overhead. Although the Canadian role was essentially defensive, Alderson saw the need to maintain an ascendency over the Germans. In a memo dated 4 March he stressed: 'Bold patrolling, persistent and accurate sniping and prompt enterprises against any sapheads.... Ambushes must be prepared, hostile patrols cut off and in fact everything done to force the conviction on the enemy that the Canadian Division is his superior.'[13] The Canadians quickly fell into the routine of trench warfare. The first few days were uneventful but on 10 March the British front, next to them, flared into action. It was the start of the Battle of Neuve Chapelle. Before continuing it is important to look at major military factors that

40

MAJOR-GENERAL R.W. TURNER

affected this battle and the upcoming Second Battle of Ypres.

At the beginning of 1915 General Joffre had evolved a plan aimed at severing the huge German bulge between Reims and Arras. He asked the British to attack in the direction of Aubers Ridge while the French Tenth Army, immediately on their right, advanced between Arras and Lens. The joint movement in the north was to synchronize with and support Joffre's own offensive in Champagne. Sir John French agreed to co-operate for he wished not only to assist his ally, but to foster an offensive spirit in the British Army after its trying and enervating winter in the trenches. [14]

Sir John also consented to relieve some French formations around Ypres that were required by the Tenth Army. French was counting on the arrival of the 29th and 1st Canadian Divisions to carry out the promised relief. But the 29th, a division made up of British regular battalions from overseas garrisons, was diverted to another theatre of war and its replacement, the 46th (North Midland Territorial) would require additional training before it could be sent to the front. In these circumstances French notified Joffre that he could not deliver his attack and simultaneously extend the British line. Sir John remained adamant in spite of being told that the Tenth Army could not carry out its part in the operation without the troops at Ypres. Joffre broke the impasse when, in a fit of anger, he cancelled the French offensive in the north. Instead of abandoning his own plans as well, Sir John, for a number of reasons, not the least of which was to show that the British could fight, decided to act alone. [15]

Sir John anticipated a break-through but in retrospect it is apparent that he had neither the trained men nor the weapons to breach the German line. Prior to 1914 Britain had placed her reliance on the Royal Navy and limited the army's functions to police duties and minor landings in remote areas. The British Army had grown since the start of the global conflict but it would remain comparatively small until the first detachments of the New Armies took the field. The British Army was further handicapped by acute shortages of heavy guns and ammunition essential to wage siege warfare. Between 1906 and 1914 insufficient government funding had compelled the army to reduce its purchase of vital equipment. No belated wartime spurt could immediately overtake the consequences of pre-war neglect. It was not until the middle of 1916 that the British government was able to provide the army with the means to fight a war of position effectively.

Although the British army fought tenaciously and resourcefully on defence, it was less adept in devising effective offensive techniques.[16] One problem was that Sir John and his advisers did not obtain full value from the available weapons. Bidwell and Graham write:

They were unaware of the principle of co-operation, and did not grasp how to co-ordinate the different arms. The art of orchestrating the fire of different weapons was not studied and in consequence the close interaction between fire and manoeuvre not understood. Artillery was regarded merely as an accessory, an extra wheel for the coach. The three arms—the cavalry, infantry and artillery—as it were, 'dined at separate tables.'[17]

Another major failing of the British Command was its inability to appreciate the importance of positional warfare. It was not seen that the principle purpose for taking an objective was to establish a new fire base on it from which to continue the fire-fight with advantage. Instead the current practice encouraged infantry forces to attack a position for no better reason than the enemy was occupying it and firing at them.

Why were the army leaders baffled by the new conditions of warfare? The answer is clear. Trained during the late nineteenth century the British generals were confronted with the weapons technology of the twentieth. Rather than re-

43

evaluate the premise upon which the new war was being fought, they applied old concepts or merely improvised tactics for local battle-field situations. The costly and indecisive attacks of 1915, 1916 and 1917 might have been avoided had there existed a doctrine based on the effective use of a weapons systems and on the progressive occupation of advantageous fire-positions.

The Battle of Neuve Chapelle was the first major attempt by the British to break the German trench system.[18] The operation was entrusted to General Douglas Haig who commanded the First Army. His objective was to capture the village of Neuve Chapelle, which lay opposite his front, and then push on to Aubers Ridge, three miles farther east. The Canadians were to supply artillery fire along their entire front and be ready to advance in the event of a break-through.

At 7.30 AM on 10 March Haig's artillery opened fire signalling the beginning of the battle. When the barrage lifted 35 minutes later, the infantrymen of the First Army clambered out of their trenches and advanced on a two-mile front into no man's land. The bombardment had proven effective. The enemy's trenches were shattered and the surviving Germans were either surrendering or running away. Within 45 minutes the British were in possession of their initial objective, Neuve Chapelle. Although setbacks had occurred on both flanks the centre had torn a gap well over a mile wide and nearly a mile deep in the German lines. Because of excessive caution and poor communications the British assault was not resumed for five hours. The delay enabled the Germans to rush reinforcements to the area and hold the British gains to a minimum. By 13 March when the battle ended the British had lost 13,000 men, about the same number as the enemy.

The Canadians had not been called upon to fight in the battle and their remaining stay in the Fleurbaix sector passed without serious incident. They were relieved by the 8th British division and on the 25th and 26th marched to new billets at Estaires, five miles behind the line. Here they received daily instructions in trench fighting with emphasis on rapid entrenching, getting out of trenches, charging over cultivated ground, crossing wire entanglements and assaulting hostile lines.[19] All this activity seemed to infer that the Canadians were being groomed to take part in the next attack in the Neuve Chapelle region.

Toward the end of March developments between the French and British High Commands suddenly changed the outlook. On 24 March Joffre wrote to Sir John suggesting that combined operations be resumed in about six weeks and reiterating his request that the French IX and XX Corps be relieved in the Ypres front by British troops as quickly as possible. Replying on 1 April the British chief welcomed the opportunity to co-operate in the proposed offensive and, noting that he expected reinforcements from home later in the month, agreed to extend his front as far north as the Ypres-Poelcappelle road.[20] Lt.-Gen. Sir Herbert Plumer, whose V Corps was a component of the Second Army, assumed responsibility for the new sector. The addition of five miles to the British line meant that only the northernmost portion of the salient, extending westward from opposite Poelcappelle to the Yser Canal at Steenstraat, would remain in French hands.

Sir John had decided that the Canadian contingent should make up part of the relief force earmarked for the Ypres salient. On 1 April he issued orders transferring the Canadian Division to the Second Army, placing it under the command of the V Corps.[21] Four days later the Canadians began their march northwards and by the 7th all units had arrived in the Cassel area—some seventeen miles west of Ypres. They were scheduled to spend a week here in preparation for their new assignment.

General Smith-Dorrien inspected the Canadian infantry brigades before they left Cassel. Speaking to them afterwards the General welcomed them to his command and observed that because of his previous association with Canadians[22] he

45

considered that the Division rightfully belonged to his Army. He complimented the men on the work accomplished at Fleurbaix and intimated that they were about to take over the most vulnerable part of the British front. The Canadians, he said, would have to contend with a foe 'more truculent' than had been supposed, but he was sure they would comport themselves 'as becomes such an excellent fighting force.'[23]

On 14 April and two succeeding days the Canadians marched up from their billets. They passed smashed and broken farmhouses and cottages, through the town of Ypres and, after zig-zagging to evade battery pits, torn up mounds and cuttings in the marshy ground, reached their assigned place in the Ypres salient. The men were in good spirits. Little did they realize that within a week they would be engaged in one of the fiercest and most terrible battles in the annals of British arms.

During the last phase of semi-open warfare, the Germans had attempted to sweep down the Belgian coast and crush the flank of the attacking Allies. They came very close to achieving their objective. The British, assisted by the French, engaged in some of the most severe fighting of the war in the Ypres sector—popularly called the First Battle of Ypres (19 October—14 November). The end of the battle left the Allied line in front of Ypres in the shape of an arc of seventeen miles, stretching from Steenstraat in the north to St. Eloi in the south. On 15 November the French took over the Ypres salient and the British consolidated along a continuous front between Wytschaete and Givenchy.[1] Thereafter there was little fighting along this perimeter and both sides settled down to construct trenches and rearward defences.

The salient was about six miles deep with the town of Ypres at the centre of its base. Ypres, known as 'Wipers' to many Canadians and Britons who lived through or grew up in the shadow of the Great War, is situated in the northwest corner of Belgium, practically on the French border. It lay in a small basin and resembled the hub of a wheel, from which roads radiated like spokes to neighbouring villages.[2] Ypres was an architectural showpiece, a blend of medieval and seventeenth-century buildings highlighted by two magnificent Gothic monuments, Cloth Hall and St. Martin's Cathedral.

The town had been the outlying fortification of the port of Dunkirk and over the centuries, as French, Dutch and Spanish armies in turn trampled over the region, it had known bombardment, siege, fire and pillage.[3] In the medieval ages it attained great importance as the centre of the cloth industry and its population was said to be over 200,000. But wars, revolts and migrations drastically undermined its lucrative cloth trade. By 1914 Ypres was a sleepy provincial backwater with a population of some 17,000. It served as the market centre of a rich agricultural district and manufactured ribbons, lace and cotton. The inhabitants there lived quietly and reasonably well and for the most part were devoted Catholics.[4]

The intense German bombardment during the First Battle of Ypres had driven away most of the people and caused considerable damage to the town. A large number of buildings were intact or sustained minor damage but in places the destruction was extensive with shell holes eight to ten feet deep yawning at intervals and groups of houses reduced to piles of brick and splintered woodwork. All that remained of the celebrated Cloth Hall was its tower. The roof had disappeared, the carved walls and statues smashed and the interior woodwork destroyed by incendiary shells. The Cathedral suffered a similar fate. A fire, started by incendiary shells, destroyed most of its treasures and left the building in ruins.[5]

As the fierce fighting settled down to the routine of trench warfare many of the inhabitants returned to the town, electing to live at home rather than face the trouble of removing themselves and their belongings to a safer location. Soon workmen were busily repairing the damage done by the previous bombardment: debris was cleared, shell holes filled and houses mended. In the fields farmers tended their crops, some to within two miles of the firing line, and their cattle grazed placidly in the green pastures. The streets of Ypres were again active and military policemen kept the traffic routes clear and the crowd moving. An occasional shell would fall on the town but for the most part it was business as usual.

On the eastern side of Ypres, at a distance of three to six miles, were a semi-circle of ridges which, though gently sloping and nowhere higher then 200 feet, nevertheless dominated the town. The earlier fighting had occurred along the higher ground that ran through numerous villages, hamlets and farms. Thus both sides centred their defences around the woods, villages and farms, which were converted into redoubts with concrete blockhouses and deep wire entanglements. Around the rim of the salient, proceeding clockwise, were the little communities of Langemarck, St. Julien, Zonnebeke and Zillebeke.

A brief description of the topography of the area is necessary in order to understand its relationship to the tactics employed by both sides during the Second Battle of Ypres. Near the southern extremity of the salient lay Hill 60. From there the main ridge, rising no more than 200 feet above sea level, or 150 feet above Ypres, ran in a northerly direction for over four miles, passing through Sanctuary Wood and Broodseinde and on to Passchendaele. A series of subsidiary spurs, a mile apart and several miles long, extended to the northwest from the main ridge. These merged into the plain and formed the watershed of the muddy little streams feeding the Steenbeek, which was joined south of Langemarck by the Lekkerboterbeek. Another series of ridges were located north of Ypres between the Steenbeek and the Yser Canal. Although no more than 50 feet above the plain, they would prove to be of great tactical value. The most northerly of these was Pilckem Ridge, one mile long and the Germans' first objective in the battle fought in April 1915. Finally the Yser Canal, which passed behind Ypres and continued in a northerly direction through Steenstraat to the sea, would constitute an impediment to the rapid movement of Allied reinforcements and supplies earmarked for the salient.[6]

There was no strategic reason why Ypres and the salient should be held.[7] The Allied position could be bombarded by German artillery from each flank as well as the front. If the infantry line was broken few men would be able to escape. The Yser Canal in the rear had only several pontoon bridges. A far better defensive position would have been one on slightly higher ground just behind Ypres. But Ypres was the only remaining town of any size left unconquered in Belgium and the French and Belgians, as well as many British generals, were simply reluctant to let it go.

The French held the salient through the winter and, for

reasons already explained, turned over about two-thirds of it to the British V Corps in mid April. General Putz with two French divisions, the 87th Territorial (General Roy) and the 45th Algerian (General Quiquandon), was given the task of defending the northern end of the salient. At a point opposite Poelcappelle the French joined up with the Canadians whose line, running in a south-easterly direction, ended in front of the village of Gravenstafel. On the right of the Canadians were the other two divisions of the V Corps, the 28th and beyond it the 27th. The 28th Division manned the line as far as Polygon Wood while the 27th Division covered the southern part of the salient to a point north of Hill 60 where the trenches of the 5th Division (II Corps) commenced.

The Canadian sector was 4500 yards in length and was divided between the 2nd Brigade on the right and the 3rd Brigade on the left. Each brigade had two battalions in the line, one in support and one in divisional reserve.[8] The 1st Brigade was in corps reserve at Vlamertinghe, several miles west of Ypres.

The German line around the Ypres salient was occupied by the Fourth Army under the command of Duke Albrecht of Württemberg. Facing the 5th and 27th (British) Divisions in the south were the 30th and 39th Divisions of the XVth Corps. Then followed the XXVIIth Reserve Corps with the 54th and 53rd Reserve Divisions opposite the 28th (British) Division and, on the right, the Landwehr Brigade confronting the 2nd Canadian Brigade. Farther north stood the XXVIth Reserve Corps with the 2nd Reserve Ersatz Brigade (part of the 51st Reserve Division) facing the 3rd Canadian Brigade while the 101st Reserve Brigade (the other half of the 51st Reserve Division) and the 52nd Reserve Division opposed respectively the 45th Algerian Division as far as the Steenbeek. The shoulder of the salient, opposite the junction of the Belgian 6th Division and the French 87th Territorial, was held by the XXIIIrd Reserve Corps with the 46th and 45th Reserve Divisions in line.[9]

50

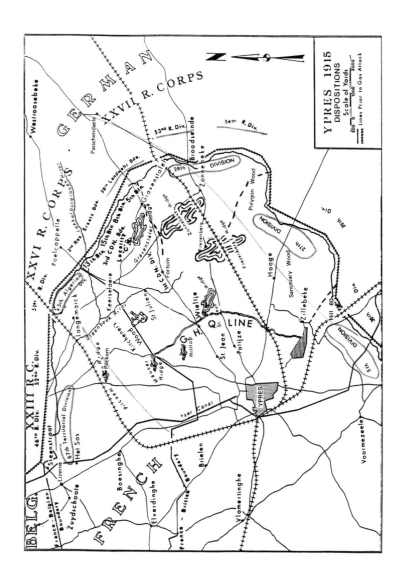

YPRES 1915
DISPOSITIONS
Scale of Yards
800 0 1000 2000
Lines Prior to Gas Attack

GERMAN

XXVII. R. CORPS
53ᴿᴰ R. Div.
54th R. Div.

XXVI R. CORPS
XXV R. C.
Westroosebeke
Passchendaele
Poelcappelle
5th R. Div.
45th Algerian Division (Langemarck Div.)

Bloodsinde
Zonnebeke
28th DIVISION
Polygon Wood
DIVISION
27th
39th Div.
Hooge
Sanctuary Wood
Zillebeke
Hill 60
5ᵀᴴ DIVISION
28ᵀᴴ DIV.

XXIII R. C.
BELG.
46ᵀᴴ R. Div.
52ᴺᴰ R. Div.
87th Territorial Division
France-Belgian Boundary
Steenstraat
Lizerne
Zuydschoote
Het Sos

FRENCH
Boesinghe
Elverdinghe
France - British Boundary
Bielen
Vlamertinghe
Voormezeele

38ᵀᴴ Landwehr Bde.
2ⁿᵈ Res. Ersatz Bde.
13ᵀᴴ Bn.
15ᵀᴴ Bn.
8ᵀᴴ Bn.
5ᵀᴴ Bn.
3rd CDN. Bde.
1ST CDN DIV.
Locality "C"
Gravenstafel
Fortuin
Zonnebeke
Frezenberg
Frezenberg Ridge

St. Julien
Kitcheners Wood
Keerselaere
Steenbeek River
Mauser Ridge
Pilckem
Hill 37
St. Jean
Wieltje
St. Julien
Potijze
G.H.Q. LINE

Yser Canal
YPRES

The Canadian division inherited a front-line defensive system that was in deplorable condition. French indifference at protecting their position was linked to their method of conducting war. It was considerably different from what the Canadians had been taught. British policy, reflecting traditional faith in the defensive ability of its infantry, mandated that front-line trenches be resolutely held. In case of enemy penetration the commanding officer was expected to counter-attack promptly and make every effort to recover the lost ground.[10] On the other hand the French, clinging zealously to the doctrine of the offensive, held forward positions with a minimum of troops. If attacked they would fall back and rely on the effective fire of their 75 mm. field guns, for which they had plenty of ammunition, to halt the enemy.

Accustomed to earthworks that conformed to British standard, the Canadians were shocked at what they saw. The lengths of trenches were shallow and unconnected, with parapets that were only about two feet high and seldom thick enough to stop bullets. There were no traverses to guard against enfilading fire, no parados to give protection from the rear. Wire entanglements and machine-gun posts were good or adequate but the dug-outs were so flimsily constructed that they offered little more than shelter from the weather.[11]

To make matters worse sanitation had been entirely disregarded. Shell holes and broken-down little side-trenches were used as latrines. Many bodies were buried in shallow graves and even in the parapet of the trenches; scores lay where they had fallen in no man's land. Large rats wandered everywhere. The line was a breeding ground for disease and the acrid smell of death permeating the air was sickening.

A 'subsidiary line' running along the crest of Gravenstafel Ridge appeared on French tactical maps but the work had been neglected and it existed merely as a series of unlinked strong points or supporting trenches. Far better prepared to resist attack than either the main or subsidiary position was the so called G.H.Q. Line (from one to three miles behind the front), which ran northwards from Zillebeke Lake to a site half a mile east of Wieltze and thence north-west to link up with the defences covering the village of Boesinghe. Built by the French, it consisted of a series of redoubts, 30 yards square and spaced about 450 hundred yards apart. The line was well situated and protected by a continuous belt of barbed wire, six yards wide and three feet high with openings only at certain roads and track crossings. Each brigade at the front was responsible for a section of the line and all regimental officers were instructed to acquaint themselves at once with the details of their position. [12]

For nearly a week every available Canadian laboured to strengthen the front-line defences. They connected isolated portions of trenches and added traverses and communication trenches. The water-table in this area was close to the surface so that trenches could not be dug to a depth of more than several feet. To acquire the desired protection there was a need to build up the parapets into breastworks of sod, mud or sandbags at least four feet high. In front of their defensive network the Canadians laid obstacles and an unbroken belt of barbed wire.

While the Canadians were hard at work, the Germans, whose trenches were only 150 to 300 yards away, made no attempt to interfere, except by occasional sniping or shelling. There was, however, an increase in enemy air activity. Some of the planes dropped bombs on the villages while others came over to assist artillery registration. Unknown to the Canadians, the relative calm was about to be broken.

Early in 1915 General von Falkenhayn, the new German supreme commander, planned a limited attack in the west as a means to cover the transfer of troops to Galacia. [13] He selected the Ypres area as the target because he proposed to use chlorine gas and it was there, the experts told him, that the winds were most favourable. The High Command was trying to find a way to break the deadlock of trench warfare as conventional methods of attack had proven ineffective. The whole idea behind the battle was to test the new weapon, to see what would happen. No large reserves had been assembled rearward in anticipation of a break-through.

There was nothing novel about the idea of utilizing toxic agents in war. The beginnings of chemical warfare are difficult to determine but one of the earliest uses was said to have occurred around 600 B.C. during the siege of Cirrha, near Delphi in Greece. According to such ancient writers as Polyaenus and Pausanias the Cirrhaeans were seized with incessant diarrhea after a drug had been dissolved in their drinking water. Thucydides has described how the Spartans tried to reduce Plataea with sulphur fumes in 429 B.C. They saturated wood with pitch and sulphur and burned it under the walls of the city so as to choke the defenders and render the assault less difficult.

These and other variants of toxic chemical warfare were employed during the middle ages. The Moors were supposed to have used acronite extracts to poison their arrow tips in their struggle against the Spaniards. In 1485 an alchemist, creating a toxic cloud by burning a chemical mixture, saved Belgrade from the attacking Turks.

Advances in chemistry in the nineteenth century led to new proposals for the employment of toxic weapons. In the midst of the US civil war a certain John W. Doughty of New York wrote to Secretary of War Edwin Stanton, recommending the use of a liquid chlorine gas shell. Stanton does not appear to have given the suggestion much, if any, consideration. [14]

The potential horrors of poison gas were recognized by the international community and at the turn of the twentieth century steps were taken to outlaw certain methods of combat. At conferences held at the Hague in 1899 and 1907 the signatories, including Germany, pledged 'to abstain from the use of projectiles the object of which is the diffusion of asphyxiating or deleterious gases.'

The Great War was barely one month old when Lord

Kitchener rejected a proposal to use incapacitating noxious gas because he felt it was ill suited for land warfare. The matter was studied during the winter of 1914-1915 and by the end of March experiments were being conducted with the view to possible employment of non-lethal gas in the Dardanelles campaign. Winston Churchill, then Lord of the Admiralty, put an end to these plans, partly out of fear that it would invite reprisals and partly out of ethical considerations posed by the Hague Conventions.[15]

The French were more advanced than the English in the development of a chemical warfare program and appear to have been the first among the belligerents to resort to toxic substances to assist their attacks. During the early weeks of the war they introduced a rifle grenade filled with bromic acid and a hand grenade filled with lachrymatory liquid called ethyl bromo-acetate. The idea was to incapacitate enemy soldiers by temporarily blinding or choking them.[16]

The question of which power initially violated the terms of the Hague Conference was a subject of charge and counter-charge during and after the Great War. German statements seem to have been based on a desire to appear in the best light. The German Official Historian claimed that by using tear-gas shells and grenades the French committed 'the first breach of international agreement in the sphere of gas warfare.'[17] Technically he may have been correct. Other German writers argued that chemical warfare, as practised by the German Army at Ypres in April 1915, did not contravene the Hague agreements. With extraordinary cynicism they attempt to make a distinction between gas delivered as drifting clouds from cylinders (the procedure adopted by the army) and gas disseminated from artillery shells. The German leaders themselves appear to have been aware that they were breaking the spirit, if not the letter, of the conventions for they made no reference to the use of poison gas in their communiqué announcing the attack at Ypres.

It is strange, some would say stupid, that the Germans

would risk, among other things, world-wide condemnation over a battlefield experiment from which no startling results were expected. There no longer is any doubt that the army generals distrusted the efficacy of toxic weapons. Their judgment was shaped not only by the traditional reluctance of the military mind to accept new methods but by the unsatisfactory results of earlier experiments.

In October 1914 the Germans had produced an artillery shell containing a charge of irritant powder, which they tried out in a local attack against the French at Neuve Chapelle. The effects were so slight that the defenders were unaware that anything out of the ordinary was being used against them. Consequently the Germans abandoned this design and began experimenting with a highly lachrymatory liquid made up of xylyl bromide and benzyl bromide. The substance was loaded in fifteen cm. howitzer shells and worked well in trials. The gas projectiles, called T-STOFF shells, were first employed against the Russians at Bolimow on 31 January, 1915, but the outcome was a fiasco. The extreme cold weather prevented the necessary evaporation of the agent and so it had no effect on the Russian troops.[18] The Germans nevertheless retained the T-STOFF shells and with some modification it would achieve improved results in better weather conditions. It was introduced on the Western Front in the French sector at Nieuport in March 1915.

Once the Germans realized the value of irritants it was only a question of time before they extended their chemical program to include lethal substances. Hastening this process was Carl Duisberg, head of I.G. Farben, a giant chemical combine in the Rhur. Duisberg was one of the first Germans to actively promote the use of poison gas. The introduction of this weapon, he foresaw, would break the stalemate and, in addition, further strengthen I.G. Farben and revive the flagging dye industry, practically at a standstill since the start of the war.[19] Duisberg was instrumental in having the matter discussed at the highest military level with the result that a decision was taken to try lethal toxic agents on the battlefield.

Initially the aim was to load the lethal chemicals into shells, as was being done with irritant agents.[20] However, owing to the limited output of projectiles at the time, the High Command doubted whether this method would create a dosage that was potent enough to affect a large area. For that reason Professor Fritz Haber, who headed the development project, suggested that chlorine be discharged from cylinders emplaced in forward trenches and propelled toward the enemy by a suitable wind. Chlorine was an agent well suited for such a technique. It was cheap, simple to produce and could easily be transported in cylinders already available because of wide industrial use.[21] When released from cylinders the gas cloud did not dissipate easily but clung to the ground as it rolled forward. Toxicologically, chlorine is a powerful irritant to the respiratory organs, causing inflammation that in turn produces a massive amount of fluid that blocks the windpipe and fills the lungs. Prolonged exposure to a high concentration of the gas causes death, or, at least, severe injury to the lungs.[22]

Haber's proposal was adopted after successful trials had been carried out. The High Command then ordered that the new weapon be tried against the Ypres salient. Haber understood the tactical value of gas. He advised his superiors to assign large reserves to exploit the break-through, which he was certain would occur.[23] But the military refused to regard the projected gas attack as anything more than a test and, in fact, did not allot any fresh reserves to support it. Duke Albrecht selected the XVth Corps' sector, opposite the south-east face of the salient, for the field experiment. Materials were accumulated; rail and road communications were extended and improved and additional accommodations were built in the forward area.

By mid February specially organized crews had finished digging in the cylinders in the XVth Corps' sector. Despite the recommendation of German meteorologists the first location proved useless because the wind consistently failed to flow from the south or south-east. During the delay additional cylinders were emplaced so that by 10 March they had been extended to cover the Corps' entire front. On 25 March Duke Albrecht ordered another battery set up further north, in the sector held by the XXVIth Reserve Corps and the 46th Reserve Division. The second front was ready by 10 April but for ten days there was no wind from the right direction.[24]

Gas cylinders were therefore present in the German front line around Ypres for over two months. During this period the Allies had ample warning of what the Germans intended to do.

Late in March prisoners (belonging to the XVth Corps) captured on the slopes of Vimy Ridge, then in the hands of the French, disclosed that the trenches north of Zillebeke held many gas cylinders, ready for use at the first favourable wind. They gave a detailed description of the method of discharge, adding that their troops had been supplied with a medicated cloth pad for protection against the gas. The local French commander placed so little faith in the report that he did not even bother to bring it to the attention of the British when they arrived to take over his front. Curiously enough particulars of the incident appeared on 30 March in the French Tenth Army bulletin, which was circulated only in the Artois district, over 100 miles away.

A fortnight later French military authorities came into possession of more concrete evidence. On 13 April a German deserter surrendered near Langemarck to the French 11th Division shortly before its relief by the Canadians. The soldier, a 24-year-old private called August Jäeger, was an automobile driver attached to the 234th Reserve Regiment, 51st Reserve Division. Under interrogation Jäeger revealed that the Germans planned to use gas and he proceeded to describe the extent of the preparations already made. Many reserve machine-gun units, light and heavy guns, 24 airplanes and a captive balloon had been recently brought into the forward area. Tubes containing asphyxiating gas were buried deeply along the front of the XXVIth Corps and fitted with rubber pipes running forward. At a given signal—three red rockets fired from an artillery position—the cylinders would be opened and the escaping gas carried toward the French trenches by a favourable wind. The gas was intended to asphyxiate the men who defended the trenches and allow the attackers to occupy them without losses. To guard against inhaling the poison gas the assaulting troops carried a packet of tow, soaked in a chemically neutralizing solution. The German deserter produced one of those crude respirators as proof of his statement.[25]

The divisional commander General Ferry, having talked to the interpreter who had interviewed Jäeger, considered the intelligence data to be of paramount importance. He at once notified General Aimé, whose 21st Brigade was in the affected sector, and prescribed the following: (1) that the number of men in the front line should be reduced; (2) that the German trenches should be shelled in order to destroy the reported cylinders; (3) that an agent be sent to warn the 28th Division and the Canadians who were due in the sector that night; (4) and that the greatest vigilance should be exercised and some means improvised to prevent gas inhalation.

At the same time Ferry sent a special messenger to the headquarters of his superior, General Balfourier, commander of the XXth Corps. By chance a liaison officer from *Grand Quartier Général* (French General Headquarters), or GQG as it was more commonly called, was there when the messenger arrived. They were shown a copy of the interrogation of the German prisoner and a list of the measures taken to meet the contingency of a gas attack. Balfourier, thinking that Ferry was a gullible fool, ignored his recommendations. GQG treated 'this gas business' as absurd and rebuked Ferry, first for bypassing usual channels to warn the British and second, for tampering with the density of the troops in the front line without regard for official policy.[26] Nor did Ferry profit when his prediction proved correct. He was dismissed from his post by General Foch who sought to cover up the bad judgment and mistakes that had preceded the battle. General Ferry's resentment over the injustice rankled until he could no longer hold his peace. In 1930 he divulged the entire story to an interested France. Ferry indiscreetly named Jäeger as the source of his information. Jäeger, now a civilian, was arrested after an investigation and brought before the Reich Supreme Court in December 1932. Found guilty of desertion and treason, he was sentenced to ten years in the penitentiary.

General Putz, who assumed charge of the northern part of the salient in mid April, was no less skeptical than his predecessor, General Balfourier. The German prisoner, on re-examination, proved so glib that Putz concluded that he was primed and sent over with the intention to deceive. Putz, in forwarding the circumstantial evidence to Smith-Dorrien's Second Army, told the British liaison officer 'that he did not believe it.'[27] Given his attitude it explains why he did not circulate the news to his own units, much less order them to take precautionary measures.

The information that the French possessed concerning German designs was supported by Belgian sources. A reliable Belgian spy sent a message over the lines to expect an attack 'with asphyxiating gas' on the Ypres salient during the night of 15-16 April.[28] (It was scheduled for that time but owing to an unfavourable wind did not take place.) On 16 April the Belgian General Staff reported that the Germans had purchased 20,000 respirators in Ghent and specifically stated that the discharge of gas would take place on the front of the XXVIth Reserve Corps.[29]

The German authorities themselves provided yet another clue. German radio broadcasts and official communiqués began making unsubstantiated allegations that the Allies were firing asphyxiating gas shells.[30] In such past circumstances the Germans had always tried to justify their behaviour by putting the blame on their opponents beforehand—like the time they falsely accused French aviators of violating German territory on 1 August, 1914. The latest charge could only mean that the Germans intended to use the new weapon.

Thus there were many signs of an impending gas attack on the north-eastern face of the Ypres salient. But GQG remained unconvinced. It had no report of fresh German reinforcements being brought up. Moreover, the night of 15-16 April passed without an attack. Finally another German deserter offered evidence that contradicted the testimony of the chauffeur.

On the morning of 15 April a former German NCO, bitter over being reduced to the ranks for striking his superior, gave himself up to the 11th (French) Division. He was a member of the 4th Landwehr Regiment (52nd Reserve Division, XXVIth Reserve Corps), which occupied the trenches between Poelcappelle Road and Passchendaele. Whatever personal grudge he may have nurtured he remained loyal to his country's cause. His replies to sensitive questions were intended to mislead his captors. He stated that there were no gas cylinders on his unit's front and that the respirator issued to him was for protection in case the Allies used asphyxiating agents.[31] The French were inclined to believe him, rather than the earlier deserter, because he had lived constantly in the trenches and because, they assumed, he had a personal score to settle with the German Army.

GQG regarded such warnings as came to its attention as a ruse, calculated to spread terror among the troops or to prevent French units from being withdrawn from Ypres to assist in the forthcoming offensive near Arras.

The British drew up contingency plans of a sort but these were sketchy. Two reserve battalions were moved closer to Ypres and units relieved from duty in the trenches were directed to remain east of the town. Air reconnaissance was intensified but failed to reveal anything unusual. Beyond this little else was done. No-one knew what kind of gas might be employed or what it would do and, through faulty reading of the evidence, it was assumed that the area threatened was clear of the British front—Jäeger had indicated that cylinders were in place on the frontage of one battalion eastwards from the Ypres-Poelcappelle road, that is opposite the left end of the Canadian line. Plumer did not attach much value to the intelligence reports and said so when he passed them on to his divisional commanders. When nothing eventful occurred on 15 April or 16 April the warnings were not only disregarded but forgotten.[32]

At no time did the British Command seriously expect the Germans to violate the rules of international warfare. Even if the unthinkable were to occur, it was supposed that the noxious gas could be fanned away or, at worst, affect only a small area that could be regained with the delivery of an immediate counter-attack.

How far down the British chain of command the warnings were passed cannot be determined. It is known that at least every Canadian brigade and battalion commander was told to expect a gas attack.[33] Beside the intelligence reports sent by Vth Corps Headquarters, there was, it can now be seen, plenty of other evidence that something was afoot. At night troops could hear the constant rumblings of wheels and gun flashes were observed nearer than usual. German airplanes came over with greater frequency, flying low to drop bombs or to register targets. Inside one such plane, brought down by French fire, was found a map showing new battery positions. While on sentry duty several soldiers (16th Battalion) noticed that pipes were being installed in the enemy's parapet and reported the incident to their superior.[34] An investigation followed but evidently uncovered nothing suspicious. Had the Canadians possessed more experience they might better have interpreted the series of warnings.

And yet Alderson had cautioned his brigade and battalion commanders to watch for a gas attack, urging them to take precautions and stand to. The degree of apprehension, however, was in general slight. At all levels of command, from Alderson downwards, the conception of gas did not convey much meaning and it was probably associated with something akin to the Chinese stinkpot. Deep down most of the high-ranking Canadian officers subscribed to the view that the stories were myths, deliberately spread by the Teutons.

A few scattered here and there took the warning seriously. Currie ordered his artillery to search for gas cylinders in the German breastworks. The exercise was unproductive as the gas cylinders were located further north.[35] Others may have tried the same counter-measures but beyond this nothing was done. Why? One explanation is that there was insufficient information and direction from above—that is, Corps and Divisional Headquarters. Victor Odlum, then second in command of the 7th Battalion, recalled after the war:

> Colonel Hart-McHarg[36] and I had an anxious talk over this [the note to expect a gas attack] ... We could not visualize an attack with gas, we could not guess where the gas would come from or how we would recognize it when it did come and we did not know what were the necessary precautions. And no-one else could tell us. So in the end, like all the others, we simply did nothing except to lay plans for action in case of an ordinary type of attack....[37]

Then too the idea existed that if noxious gas were discharged it would be localized and on the French front. Finally some believed that any reference to the new weapon would inspire terror among the men or violate instructions from the Second Army issued on 15 April, calling for reticence in dealing with secret or confidential matters. After 17 April Canadian attention was distracted by two other events.

The first was the fight for Hill 60, an artifical mound built up out of earth excavated from the cutting of the adjacent Ypres-Comines railway. Situated on the crest of the Ypres ridge, it had been captured by the Germans in December 1914. It was of considerable tactical importance since it commanded a good view of the salient, particularly toward Zillebeke and Ypres. British sappers had tunnelled under the mound and set mines containing five tons of explosives. On the evening of 17 April the mines were exploded, creating three big craters in the hill and killing most of the 150 defenders. Before the smoke had cleared away, the 13th Brigade (5th Division) rushed up the hill and took what remained of the German trenches. After midnight on the 18th the Germans counter-attacked and reached the British position before being driven back with the bayonet. For the next three days there was no let-up in the fighting.[38] Early on the 21st the 1st Canadian Brigade, released from army reserve, was placed at the disposal of the 5th Division and ordered to be prepared to move to Hill 60 at an hour's notice. The routes to the forward area were reconnoitred and the morning of the 22nd found the 2nd and 4th Battalions standing by. Before the day was over the 1st Brigade would find itself in action but not on Hill 60.

The second was the violent bombardment of Ypres, which began 20 April. The object of the Germans was to block the routes through which the Allies supplied their forces in the salient. Huge 42 cm. shells rained upon the town, remorselessly grinding away streets and buildings and killing scores of civilians.[39] The British interpreted the German action as nothing more than retaliation for the loss of Hill 60. They were wrong. It was the prelude to an attack.

The orders for the gas attack were issued on 8 April but they could not be carried out until the late afternoon of the 22nd when the direction of the wind was right. Because the High Command had doubts as to what the gas could accomplish, it had set limited objectives. On the XXIIIrd Reserve Corps' front the 45th Reserve Division would capture Steenstraat while the 46th Reserve secured the line of the Yser Canal with bridgeheads at Het Sas and Boesinghe. Both divisions would then co-operate in seizing Lizerne. Simultaneously, on the left, the 51st Reserve Division was to take Langemarck and the 52nd Reserve (both of the XXVIth Reserve Corps) Pilckem. The attainment of these goals, it was felt, would compel the Allies to abandon the salient.[40]

The attack on the 22nd was originally set for 5.45 AM. Everything was ready. Respirators were examined to see if they were damp; cylinder tubes were laid over the parapet; and passages cut in the wire. The troops, with bayonets fixed, were scheduled to go over the top ten minutes after the gas had been released. But there was not a breath of wind that morning and at 5.30 AM the operation was postponed. The men, in full gear and packed in together, were forced to remain in the trenches most of the day. Toward the end of the afternoon a north breeze sprang up and orders were given to start the attack at 5 PM.[41] Accordingly 180,000 kilograms of chlorine were discharged from 5730 cylinders along a three and three-quarter miles front, from Steenstraat on the Yser Canal to a point east of Langemarck (near Poelcappelle). For unknown reasons the cylinders south of Poelcappelle remained sealed.[42] Behind the gas long lines of German infantry mounted their parapets and began to advance.

22 April was a pleasant sunny day with an occasional light wind and the temperature in the seventies. Throughout the morning the Germans had directed the fire of their seventeen-inch and eight-inch howitzers on Ypres and the nearby towns but by early afternoon all was quiet. Air reconnaissance revealed considerable activity behind the German lines, especially in the Houthulst Forest where a column was seen marching. But there was nothing abnormal in this sort of thing, at least not enough to cause apprehension at Divisional or Corps Headquarters.

The daily routine of the troops of the 1st Canadian Division continued uninterrupted. The 1st Brigade at Vlamertinghe, although alerted for possible action at Hill 60, carried on with training. Two battalions of the 3rd Brigade, the 13th and 15th, had worked hard all night, filling sandbags, building breastworks, digging and repairing barbed-wire entanglements. These battalions occupied the left of the Canadian line, next to the Zouave and Turco troops of the French 45th Division. The 14th Battalion was in support near the village of St. Jean, a short distance away, and the 16th Battalion was in reserve outside Ypres.

On the right the 8th and 5th Battalions of the 2nd Brigade carried the Canadian line until it joined with the 28th Division. These 2nd Brigade units, like the 13th and 15th Battalions, were busy shoring up defensive works. The 7th Battalion was in support nearby (at the village of Fortuin) and the 10th Battalion was in reserve near Ypres. Reserve and support battalions typically looked for ways to pass the time. One officer put in a request for some playing-cards and mouth-organs.[1] Another made arrangements to conduct a cock-fight, a popular local diversion novel to most Canadians.

Soon after 4 PM the Germans unleashed a furious bombardment on the French positions along the north of the salient.

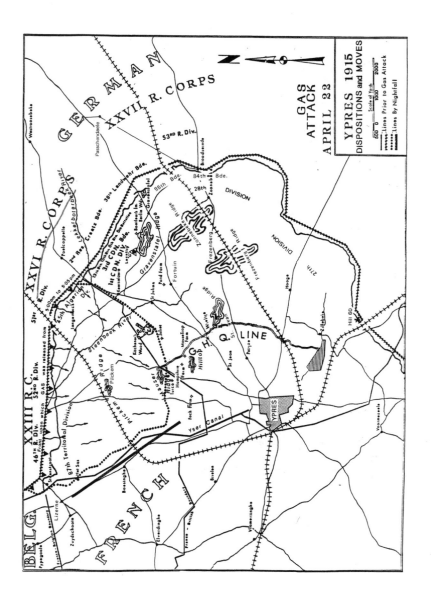

YPRES 1915
DISPOSITIONS and MOVES

GAS
ATTACK
APRIL 22

Scale of Yards
500 0 1000 2000

Lines Prior to Gas Attack
Lines By Nightfall

The range gradually lengthened to include the Canadian trenches, then the nearby roads, villages and Ypres itself. French field guns replied and kept firing even after German artillery had ceased.[2] Around 5 PM, as word was passed along the Canadian line that the Germans were attacking the French, left companies of the 3rd Brigade noticed that the sun had a peculiar greenish appearance.[3] Those on points of vantage (amongst them General Alderson who was visiting a battery unit) saw two greenish-yellow clouds drifting slowly across no man's land, on either side of Langemarck. The clouds spread laterally until they united into one long low bank of fog and, under the impulsion of a light breeze, rolled down on the trenches of the Algerian Division.[4] The French troops in this sector were not of the highest quality and they had no inkling that the enemy might employ poison gas. Clutching their throats and mad with agony hundreds died of suffocation while hundreds more lay helpless, froth on their lips, their bodies periodically racked with searing nausea. Their morale broken by this unknown terror the rest, half asphyxiated, with eyes streaming and nose and throat burning, sought to escape toward the rear. The gas and panic spread to the Territorials and they too joined in with their fleeing comrades. Those who fled found that they could not outdistance the deadly fumes. Later it was estimated that the gas travelled six miles an hour, as fast as most soldiers could run.

Singly or in groups the French infantrymen stumbled across fields, through hedges, over ditches and down the roads in the direction of the canal bridges. Many did not halt their flight until they reached Ypres or crossed over to Vlamertinghe and put the canal between themselves and their diabolical enemies.[5] Canadian units, in the path of the retreat, were amazed at the sight of the panic-stricken rabble of Turcos and Zouaves with their reeking yellowed clothing and ashen purple faces twisted and distorted by pain, pointing at their throats and vainly trying to gain relief by vomiting.[6]

The fugitives were incoherent and it was impossible to understand what they said but from their appearance it was evident that they were terrified. Behind them came stragglers from the 87th Territorial Division sobbing hysterically '*la guerre est finie! La guerre est finie.*'[7] Then, almost simultaneously, the onlookers sniffed something in the air, something which brought tears to their eyes and caught at the back of their throats, filling their mouths with a metallic taste.

Lt.-Col. G.G. Nasmith, an analytical chemist, was one of the first, if not the first, to determine the nature of the gas. A native of Toronto, the 4'6" Nasmith had been ruled ineligible for combat service on account of his diminutive stature. But he was enthusiastic and eager to help in some capacity. His persistence paid off for eventually he received authority from the Minister of Militia to organize a laboratory in order to test and clear the drinking water of the Canadian troops overseas.[8]

On 22 April Nasmith, on his way to the salient, stopped at an Advanced Dressing-Station at Wieltze where he ran into his old friend Captain F.A.C. Scrimger, Medical Officer of the 14th Battalion. Having left the car at the edge of the village, the two men were walking toward the trenches when they saw a long cloud of dense yellowish-green smoke rising and drifting in their direction. 'That must be the poison gas we have heard vague rumours about,' Nasmith remarked. As the gas continued to ascend and expand Nasmith noticed that here and there the yellowish-green clouds were streaked with brown. 'It looks like chlorine,' he said and Scrimger agreed that it probably was.[9] Half an hour later the gas reached them, making them cough and causing tears to stream down from their eyes. Nasmith inclined to believe that the gas was essentially chlorine, with perhaps an admixture of bromine, but he was uncertain whether the irritation to their eyes had been caused by the presence of another agent.

On reaching his laboratory he conducted a series of tests and determined that the gas was 'largely chlorine but with probably some bromine present.' The next day he wrote directly to Divisional Headquarters, bypassing the normal channels in order to save time. He revealed his findings and suggested, as the best means to protect the men, the use of a pad soaked in hyposulphite of soda. On 28 April a team of prominent chemists, brought over from Britain in haste, confirmed Nasmith's analysis and identified the same antidote that he had recommended five days before. [10]

The Canadians, witnessing the gruesome effect of poison gas on the Algerians, were naturally distressed but almost to a man they remained astonishingly calm. Fifty years later, Andrew McNaughton, a former artillery officer, explained: 'Somehow we felt it was the normal course of war. It was unpleasant, it's true, but nobody got very excited about it. Now later on, when we'd learned a little about war, we wouldn't have been there at all; we'd have been off within the next couple of hours.' [11] Other survivors spoke in similar terms:

Victor Odlum: 'Fortunately we were neither alarmed nor excited. Had this event occurred later in the war, when we knew more, we might have been both.' [12]

Elliot Green: 'If they were better troops they would have withdrawn immediately and if they'd been worse troops, they wouldn't be there at all—they'd have panicked.' [13]

George Patrick: 'No-one had any idea of getting out. We didn't know enough about it to know that we were licked. We went in there and we were going to stay there, and that was that.' [14]

The chlorine concentration almost completely covered the sector occupied by the 45th Algerian and 87th Territorial Divisions but did not penetrate the Canadian zone in strength. Even so some Canadian gunners, whose artillery was near the French boundary, suffered from the effects of the gas. 'We weren't equipped with gas masks,' recalled a member of the 9th Field Battery. 'Men were coughing, spitting and choking, and we didn't know what to do till the MO of the 14th Battalion, Captain Scrimger, was rushing up and down telling everyone to urinate on your pocket handkerchief, tie it over your mouth, and he saved thousands of lives.'[15]

As if by magic two French divisions had practically disappeared. Unaffected by the gas, only the right of the 1/1st Tirailleurs, next to the 13th Canadian Battalion, remained in position as did the 1/2nd bis Zouaves, who were in support. Between Steenstraat and what remained of the 45th Algerian there was a four-mile breach in the Allied line. Long waves of German infantrymen, with crude respirators over their faces, advanced behind and sometimes through the gas, methodically shooting and bayoneting any French troops that stirred.

Chaos reigned behind the front. Shells fell incessantly and with mathematical precision on Ypres, turning the town into a flaming inferno. Children wailed, men cursed and growled and women cried for loved ones buried under the collapsed buildings or mangled by the shells. For N. Nicholson of the 16th Battalion not even the passing of a half-century could dim the recollection of that horrifying spectacle: 'People were screaming and running hither and thither. As a matter of fact, I saw one woman carrying a baby and the baby's head was gone, and it was quite devastating.'[16] Forced out of their homes the townsfolk trudged down the streets, almost numbed and paralyzed by terror. Some drove their animals before them, others helped the elderly or carried children and still others pushed carts laden with their most cherished belongings. Outside of Ypres this sad procession mingled with the passing stream of equally terrified soldiers, horse-drawn waggons, lorries and field batteries. The roads leading westward from the town were so congested that any coherent movement of troops to the front was practically impossible.

The sounds of the German bombardment and the initial

reply by the French 75s and rifle fire, followed by the penetrating stench of the chlorine, alerted Canadian Divisional Headquarters that something serious was going on. For several hours it was impossible to ascertain precisely what had occurred because of the completeness of the French collapse and the disruption of the telephone lines by artillery fire. In the meantime unit commanders were issuing quick, independent orders in an effort to combat the strange menace that was developing to the north.

The first Canadian infantry unit to engage the enemy in close combat was the 13th Battalion. The effects of the German bombardment on the 13th had been severe, not as much on the front line as on the rear support trenches occupied by Major E.C. Norsworthy and two platoons of No. 3 Company. After sustaining a number of casualties Norsworthy, who was second in command of the battalion, notified Major D.R. McCuaig of No. 1 Company that he was withdrawing his men a short distance but that he would remain ready to move up in support should the companies at the front require assistance. A few minutes later the telephone line was cut and direct connection with the rear was lost. McCuaig found himself in command of the three companies in the front line —Nos. 1, 2 and 4. The remaining two platoons of No. 3 Company were in St. Julien with the battalion commander Lt.-Col. F.O.W. Loomis.

Around 5 PM McCuaig, worried by reports that the French were under heavy attack and unable to account for the sun's peculiar greenish tint, went over to investigate, taking a platoon with him. As he made his way into the continuous trench of the 1st Tirailleurs he found them holding a breastwork, running at right angles from their original line, exchanging a brisk fire with Germans occupying a parallel hedge 150 yards away. Insufficient cover prevented McCuaig from extending the French line further to the rear so he took a position in echelon in the ditch along the east side of the Poelcappelle road. There he was soon joined by a second platoon and then part of a third.[17]

McCuaig does not appear to have realized the extent of the French debacle and the seriousness of his own position until around 6 PM when a salvo from a battery scored four direct hits on his trenches, causing a dozen or more casualties. All indications were that the Germans, presumably using a captured gun, were firing from his left rear. McCuaig concluded, correctly as it turned out, that the Germans had swung in toward the Canadian flank and were heading in the general direction of St. Julien. He was less certain whether anything could be done in time to stop them. Indeed, apart from hasty dispositions made from within the resources of the Canadian Division, the left flank of the Second Army lay open to the Yser Canal.

South and a little to the rear of McCuaig's front, at a distance of 700 or 800 yards, lay the two support platoons of No. 3 Company. Norsworthy's Highlanders, augmented by a few Algerian riflemen driven back by the gas, lined the ditch on the west side of the Poelcappelle road. Between this small outpost and St. Julien there existed, except for the 10th Field Battery below Keerselaere, an unguarded stretch of more than a mile.

The battalion commander, Lt.-Col. Loomis, had the added responsibility of defending St. Julien. Besides the two platoons of No. 3 Company (13th Battalion) he had at his disposal No. 2 Company of the 14th and No. 2 Company of the 15th. At 5 PM he ordered his force into battle, sending No. 2 Company of the 14th and No. 2 Company of the 15th to occupy trenches north of the village and holding the remaining two platoons in reserve.[18]

Half a mile to the west a British 4.7-inch battery in Kitchener's Wood[19] constituted the only protection for the wide opening between St. Julien and 3rd Brigade Headquarters at Mouse Trap Farm. This gap presented a greater danger than the one north of the village as it was closer to the centre of the German attack. At. 6 PM Turner ordered the 14th Battalion (less one company, which was in St. Julien), in reserve at St. Jean, to occupy a stretch of the GHQ Line, from the Ypres-St. Julien road to beyond Mouse Trap Farm.[20] On the left of the 14th Battalion about 500 Zouaves defended the trenches as far westward as Hampshire Farm while on its right the 3rd Field Company covered the Wieltje-St. Julien road.

The fate of the British in the salient would surely have been sealed if the Germans had adopted more sensible tactics during the Second Battle of Ypres. On the 22nd and during succeeding days the Germans were content to take short steps forward, relying on their artillery and gas to clear the way to lines selected beforehand. The High Command resorted to limited objectives because the available infantry was insufficient in numbers and too inferior in quality to obtain a decision by mere weight of attack. Such deliberate methods of advance proved successful under different circumstances later in the war. But when speed was vital, as was the case at Second Ypres, they were a prescription for failure.

The German assault on 22 April began well with both corps speedily gaining their objectives, except on the canal flank. On the front of the 45th Reserve Division, opposite Steenstraat, a number of gas cylinders were not discharged for reasons that have never been explained. Only late in the evening and after considerable losses was the village taken. The adjoining 46th Division crossed the canal and captured Het Sas but its left was held up east of Boesinghe. The two divisions of the XXVIth Reserve Corps penetrated even deeper. The 52nd Reserve Division broke through unchecked and by 5.40 PM had reached its first objective, Pilckem Ridge. Farther east the 51st Reserve Division encountered fierce resistance at Langemarck, perhaps because the garrison there had escaped the full effects of the gas fumes. Nevertheless the 51st was in possession of Langemarck by 6 PM and its commander was ordered to cross the Steenbeck, and if possible, seize St. Julien.[21]

Within an hour the left wing of the 51st Reserve Division was brushing against the flank of the 3rd Canadian Brigade. The way was clear on the right and the Germans pushed forward rapidly, occupying the trenches south of Kitchener's Wood. It was a different matter on the other side. We have already noted that McCuaig and his Highlanders, in coming to the assistance of the 1st Tirailleurs, were holding their own against what was obviously a vastly superior force. Around 9 PM the Germans made a more concerted effort, driving the Algerians from their isolated breastwork. The Canadians were able to rally some 200 of them and used them to reinforce the line along the Poelcappelle road or to assist in building a parados for the original front trench where the absence of proper protection had caused heavy losses.

Throughout the night of 22-23 April McCuaig was faced with a myriad of problems that would have tested the resourcefulness of a much more experienced officer. His communications had been cut, he was without artillery support and his men were suffering severely from heavy enfilading fire. By all the rules of war he was a beaten man and, as such, should have retired. But he stubbornly held on. By doing so he apparently deceived the Germans into thinking that behind him lay a much larger force which, of course, was not the case.

Further south the Germans ran into Norsworthy and his men near the Lekkerboterbeek crossing. The two Canadian platoons and the handful of Algerians, inspired by the gallant leadership of Norsworthy, put up a fierce struggle, thwarting several attempts by the enemy to work around McCuaig's rear.[22] Their backs to the wall they refused to surrender and fought on with mounting casualties until overwhelmed by sheer weight of numbers. Norsworthy was killed in hand-to-hand combat and the few that survived were taken prisoner.

As the Germans swept triumphantly toward St. Julien they were unaware that the Canadian 10th Field Battery was

75

deployed in an orchard just south of Keerselaere. This unit had, since the start of the battle, been firing steadily in support of the 13th Battalion. The early spring light had begun to fade when the battery commander, Major W.B. King, saw scores of Algerians fleeing down the road. While trying to rally them a French sergeant gripped his arm, pointed to a hedge on the west side of the road and cried 'Allemand.' King turned and to his amazement saw over the hedge the spiked helmets of a large column of German infantry, which he judged to be no more than 300 yards away, marching in the direction of St. Julien. King hastened back to his battery position and ordered a section of his guns to swing 90 degrees to the left. At point blank range the gunners fired over open sights. The Germans provided the sort of target that gunners dream of and within a few minutes their dead lay in heaps on the ground. The survivors turned and ran, taking cover some distance away. After digging themselves in they directed a steady rifle fire at the Canadian gunners, bringing down showers of willow leaves from the nearby trees.[23]

As the battery was in an exposed position, King requested help from the St. Julien garrison. Loomis at once sent a covering party of 60 infantrymen as well as a machine-gun detachment. The infantry entrenched near the battery while the machine-gun team, led by nineteen-year-old Corporal Frederick Fisher of Montreal, moved forward under heavy fire. Fisher set up the Colt gun in an isolated building, which enjoyed a commanding view over the enemy, and brought it into effective action. All four members of his crew were hit but, as they fell, they were replaced by others nearby. With eager hands feeding the belts of ammunition into the breech, Fisher continued to work the gun, spraying and ripping the enemy's front. His skill and daring, for which he was awarded the Victoria Cross, contributed immeasurably to the safe withdrawal of the 10th Battery's guns. Unfortunately Fisher never lived to wear the prized medal. He was killed in action the next day.[24]

Back at Divisional Headquarters such information as trickled in from the front was often unclear or inaccurate. General Alderson who, as we saw earlier, was near St. Julien when the attack started, returned on foot to his horse. He then rode back to his headquarters, in the Chateau des Trois Tours (west of Brielen), arriving shortly before 6 PM. The first reports were already in. One from the Second Brigade indicated that its front had not been attacked.[25] Another from the 3rd Brigade advised that an attack had been launched against the French to the north.[26] No further news of importance came to hand until receipt of a series of telegrams, brought by messenger from 3rd Brigade Headquarters, conveyed an entirely wrong impression of the condition of the Canadian flank.

6.25 PM   Left of our left subsection is retiring.[27]
6.45 PM   Your wire to us is down. Our left driven back and apparently whole line forced back toward St. Julien.[28]
7.10 PM   We are forced back on GHQ Line. Attack coming from west. No troops left. Need ammunition badly. Have asked 2nd Bde to support.[29]

Alderson, having relayed this faulty intelligence to the V Corps, urged upon the 2nd and 3rd Brigades the need to stand their ground.[30] He directed one of his divisional reserve battalions, the 16th, to report to General Turner.[31] The other, the 10th, was given similar orders[32] but, as it was held up by the stream of fugitives, turned into the GHQ Line east and south-east of Wieltje. In response to Turner's plea for help Currie, whose headquarters were at Pond Farm, south-east of St. Julien, placed the 7th Battalion on alert. An hour and a half later, as a precautionary move, Currie ordered the 7th to a strong point known as 'Locality C' where it occupied a supporting position behind the junction of the 2nd and 3rd Brigades.

The first report of a gas attack did not reach Second Army Headquarters until 6.45 PM, although General Smith-Dorrien, who was returning on foot to Ypres after visiting Hill 60, had himself observed the cloud moving toward the French lines. At 7.45 PM two messages arrived, indicating that a disaster had occurred. The first told of the French retirement and the second erroneously reported that the left of the 3rd Canadian Brigade had been forced back to Wieltje. Subsequently General Putz confirmed that the enemy had used asphyxiating gas, adding incorrectly that his right was at Pilckem. This meant that a gap of over 3000 yards had been forced open between the French and the Canadians. Currie, recalling a conversation he had with Smith-Dorrien early in May 1915, wrote:

> He told me that when he first heard of the gas attack and retirement of the French Colonial troops he threw up his hands and foresaw the greatest disaster that ever overtook the British Army. He said that if every man in the salient had tried to get out that night he would not have blamed them, and when he pictured all the men, guns and transport crossing the few bridges over the canal, with a victorious army thundering at their heels, he shuddered. Then, he said he got a message that the Canadians were holding on. At first he refused to believe it and sent his own staff officer to verify the report.[33]

As a first step toward re-establishing the line, Smith-Dorrien released the 1st Canadian Infantry Brigade from army reserve and placed it at the disposal of the V Corps. Plumer, whose headquarters were at Poperinghe, in turn, handed back half the brigade, the 2nd and 3rd Battalions, to Alderson.[34] At the same time Plumer turned over to Alderson the 2nd East Yorkshires, then in hutments a mile northwest of Ypres. This unit, which formed part of the 28th Division's reserve, was the first of 33 British battalions to come under Alderson's command during the battle.

By 8.45 PM V Corps Headquarters had received sufficient information to conclude that both of Putz's divisions had been driven from their first and second lines of defence with the loss of all their guns and that there were no formed bodies of French troops east of the canal except at Steenstraat. A glance at the map showed that the gap was not 3000 yards but 8000, providing the enemy with a clear path to menace Ypres and take in the rear the three British divisions still holding the salient. It was clear to Plumer that other reserves had to be found before such a threat developed into an overwhelming disaster.

Alderson's counterparts on the right, Generals T.D'O. Snow and E.S. Bulfin, who commanded, respectively, the 27th and 28th Divisions, had grasped the fact that, except for a few Canadian dispositions scattered here and there, the Second Army's left flank lay open. Without waiting for orders these two divisional commanders dispatched some of their reserves to the threatened flank. The 27th Division moved the 4th Battalion and the 2nd KSLI (King's Shropshire Light Infantry) to the St. Jean-Potijze area. The 28th Division contributed four battalions. The 2nd East Kents, more familiarly known as the Buffs, and the 3rd Middlesex, in billets and bivouacs near St. Jean, marched to the ridge north of the village and deployed westward as far as the Yser Canal. The 1st York and Lancaster Regiment, in reserve west of Ypres, was called forward to reinforce St. Jean. The 5th King's Own Royal Regiment was held in reserve. All four battalions would soon come under the orders of the senior officer, Colonel A.D. Geddes of the Buffs, and for the next five days fought at the disposal of the Canadian Division. It should be pointed out that the composition of Geddes' force varied almost from day to day and for convenience may be referred to as 'Geddes' Detachment.'[35]

As the various British units marched toward their allocated places, Alderson received a hand-delivered note from

3rd Brigade Headquarters.[36] In it Turner reported that the rumours his brigade had been forced back were erroneous and that the original line was still in place. This was good news but the situation remained highly dangerous. The left flank of the Second British Army ended abruptly just west of Mouse Trap Farm and in the whole of this distance only three points were held: McCuaig, with several hundred Highlanders and Tirailleurs, occupied a ditch at the northern end; two and a half companies under Loomis covered St. Julien; and the 14th Battalion was in the vicinity of Mouse Trap Farm. These dispositions left unguarded three great gaps of 2000 yards, 1000 yards and 3000 yards. Even after the arrival of reinforcements it was hard to see how the new flank, unprotected by wire and with only makeshift trenches, could possibly maintain a prolonged resistance.

Suddenly, with victory practically in their grasp, the Germans halted their drive. Von Falkenhayn, underestimating the effects of the new weapon, had not provided the means to convert the break-in into a break-through. Only one division was available in army reserve and when released the next day, was given to the XXIIIrd Reserve Corps, not the XXVIth, which had made the deepest penetration. There had been no arrangements to carry out special tactical training for the troops following up the gas cloud. The attacking infantrymen advanced two miles when they stumbled into their own poisoned fumes and cautiously held back. They had only been issued crude respirators, which many had not bothered to wear owing to the difficulty in breathing. Passing through the French trenches they were struck by the unprecedented scene of horror and apparently became concerned about their own safety. The fear of gas, together with the high-spirited stand of the Canadians, made the Germans only too willing to stop and dig in as soon as they had reached their assigned objectives.[37] In doing so they failed to discover the extent of their success and the weakness of the Canadian line hastily thrown in the path of their flank. And on the days that followed they showed the same lack of ardour, merely moving forward to occupy the patches of ground that their artillery and gas had practically swept free of defenders. If the Germans had pressed their advantage on the 22nd there is every likelihood that the Ypres salient, with its garrison numbering upwards of 50,000 men and 150 guns, would have fallen.

As darkness fell and enemy pressure slackened, the wounded started to arrive from the front in large numbers. Regimental Aid Posts had been set up behind the lines, at locations visually screened from artillery observers or snipers, and as far as possible equi-distant from each of the companies at the front. At each RAP a Medical Officer with an NCO and several orderlies attended to the wounded as they walked in or were brought by stretcher-bearers. The RAP was not a place where delicate surgery was performed but rather it was a sort of casualty ward. Here the medical staff bandaged wounds, applied splints to fractured limbs, arrested bleeding and injected morphine to dull the pain of serious injuries.

After the patients received first aid, the immediate goal was to remove them out of the fire zone as rapidly as possible. From the RAP the wounded were taken to the Advanced Dressing Station, which was situated within the fire zone at some place along the road. Ambulances came up—if not always feasible during the day then at night—to convey the disabled to the next relay point, the Main Dressing Station. Here they were classified according to the nature of their injury. Severe cases were operated on immediately and kept at the MDS until they were fit to be transferred to the Casualty Clearing Station. Patients with superficial wounds were given rest and treatment for a few days and sent either back to their units or to a convalescent camp in the neighbourhood. Those requiring specialized surgery were transferred to other hospitals.

The Casualty Clearing Station was well behind the firing line and always situated in the vicinity of a railhead. Its primary function was to provide the immediate post-operative care. The patients were then placed aboard an ambulance train and carried to the base, the final stage in their journey.

The medical system, hitherto untried in actual warfare, proved itself elastic and adaptable and such defects as appeared under the sudden and intense strain of battle were generally remedied in a few hours. For everyone concerned the early days of the Second Battle of Ypres were a nightmare. As the wounded continued to pour into the aid stations additional accommodations were sought in adjoining houses and in billets of nearby army units. The clearing of the wounded was no less urgent and everything imaginable was used for transport—horse-drawn vehicles, motor lorries, omnibuses, village carts and gun limbers. Doctors and the medical staff laboured by the dim light of lamps and candles and in spite of their unremitting work the long rows of stretcher cases in the court yards never seemed to diminish. Frequently aid stations were forced to move on account of enemy shelling.

It is not known exactly how many wounded passed through the hands of the Canadian Army Medical Corps throughout the first week of the Second Battle of Ypres. No. 3 Field Ambulance alone treated some 5200 cases. Since the start of the war probably no other unit of the British Army attended to as many wounded during a comparable period as did the Canadian Army Medical Corps. In sum both men and system stood the test of war and abundantly showed their quality.[38]

At 8 PM on 22 April, before it became known that the Germans had halted, a French liaison officer arrived at Alderson's Headquarters with a request from General Putz for Canadian assistance in a counter-attack that the 45th Division was preparing to launch toward Pilckem. One can only speculate why such an appeal was made in view of Putz's clear inability to keep his end of the proposal. The Algerian Division was in no position to attack as it had lost all its artillery and was in terrible disarray. This was unknown to Alderson who felt that concerted pressure on both sides of the breach might compel the enemy to withdraw. Accordingly Alderson ordered Turner to clear Kitchener's Wood and then, in co-operation with the French, direct his advance slightly east of Pilckem. Turner was told to begin his counter-attack as soon as his reinforcements had arrived.

Although the instructions were issued at 9.40 PM it was not until midnight that the troops for the purpose, the 10th and 16th Battalions, were ready to move out. The 16th was late in reporting, having been held up by the fugitives. For a time 3rd Brigade Headquarters feared that the 10th Battalion would have to go in alone.

The two battalions, with the 10th (Lt.-Col. R.L. Boyle) in the lead and the 16th (Lt.-Col. R.G.E. Leckie) in close support, advanced in column of half battalion. That is, the four companies of the 10th, divided into half companies 30 yards apart, marched shoulder-to-shoulder in four waves at 30-yard intervals. The 16th, 30 yards in the rear, was in the same for-mation except the distance between each line was twenty yards.[39] The 1500 man force had 100 bombers and was covered by the 9th and 12th Batteries firing on the northern part of the wood and beyond.

The assault to retake Kitchener's Wood was the only counter-attack mounted during the Second Battle of Ypres that was operationally sound in its conception. The Canadi-ans were not expected to attack and under cover of night would retain the element of surprise until practically the moment of impact. The Germans had neither strength of numbers nor time to prepare fixed defences. Then too, the objective was well chosen. The capture of Kitchener's Wood would deny the Germans of an obvious jumping off place for further attacks; and cause them to interrupt their advance or risk a British build up inside their left flank.

While the venture was sound militarily, its planning and execution were deplorable. There was no prearranged set of objectives. The men were deployed in a formation that may have been suitable for early nineteenth-century warfare but certainly not after the invention of the magazine rifle and machine-gun. On top of this the enemy's exact location was unknown so that the 1500 Canadian troops would be advancing blindly toward a dark blur.

At 11.45 PM, five minutes before the 9th and 12th Canadian artillery batteries opened fire on the northern part of the wood, a brigade major gave the official order to advance. With bayonets fixed and rifles at the port the Canadians moved forward, only the steady tramp of 3000 feet and the slap of empty scabbards against the thighs could be heard. The men had covered half the distance to the wood when the leading wave stumbled into a hedge and a wire fence. The noise alerted the enemy. Suddenly a shower of flares lit up the countryside and the Canadians, bunched up as they were, became an ideal target. As enemy machine-guns ripped out and rifles crackled the Canadians fell in swaths. The ranks wavered and swayed for an instant but encouraged by their officers—in particular Captain John Geddes of the 16th, a former football player, who, although mortally wounded struggled valiantly on hands and knees shouting 'Come on! Come on!'—they recovered their balance and with a wild and ear-shrieking cry surged forward. They poured into the enemy's trench, which ran along the southern edge of the wood, and captured it with rifle butt and bayonet. A few minutes later the attackers pressed on into the wood.[40]

Here it was so dark that the men could not see more than a few feet in front of them. Marching over unknown ground, the units lost direction and cohesion after encountering scattered groups of Germans. One participant graphically described what happened:

The struggle became a dreadful hand-to-hand conflict; we fought in clumps and batches, and the living struggled over the bodies of the dead and dying. At the height of the conflict, while we were steadily driving the Germans

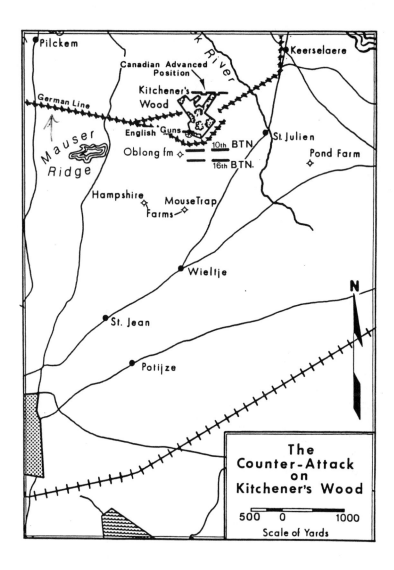

The Counter-Attack
on
Kitchener's Wood

500   0   1000
Scale of Yards

before us, the moon burst out. The clashing bayonets flashed like quicksilver, and faces were lit up as by limelight. Sweeping on, we came upon lines of trenches that had been hastily thrown up and could not be stubbornly defended. Here all who resisted were bayoneted; those who yielded were sent to the rear.[41]

The two Canadian battalions, having fought their way slightly beyond the northern fringes of the wood, halted and entrenched themselves. Now trouble developed in the rear. The sound of musketry fire was punctuated by a shout in good English, 'We have you surrounded: surrender.'[42] The demand was ignored but an investigation showed that this came from a German redoubt at the south-western extremity of the wood, about fifteen yards from the captured trench. A mixed party of 34 Canadians were detailed to deal with the stronghold. But enemy fire proved insurmountable and after half the attacking force had fallen the remainder drew back and began to dig a cross trench to cover the flank.

Subsequently it was discovered that the redoubt was part of a strongly held trench-system extending westward. East of the wood, on the opposite flank, the Germans were in force and touch could not be established with the garrison in St. Julien. There was, moreover, continued rifle fire from the north-west, indicating that the enemy still occupied that corner of the wood.

During the charge the two Canadian battalions had suffered staggering casualties. The 10th was able to muster only five officers and 188 other ranks out of more than 800 men. Lt.-Col. Boyle died from multiple bullet wounds and his second in command, Major MacLaren, also hit, was killed by a shell while on his way to the hospital.[43] The 16th had lost its adjutant and three company commanders. Only five officers and 260 other ranks were able to answer the roll.[44]

Around 1 AM Leckie dispatched a message to 3rd Brigade Headquarters. He reported that the wood had been carried and four British guns recovered—these had been lost when the wood was overrun by the Germans in their first rush. He requested reinforcements to secure his flank and a team of horses to remove the guns.[45]

The position now held by the Canadians in the wood was 1000 yards behind the enemy's line.[46] Whether they could maintain control over all the ground regained was another matter. The anticipated French attack on the left had not taken place. The absence of a post-battle plan, the intermingling of units and the losses, especially among the officers, hampered consolidation. Further difficulties were created by the enemy's tremendous concentration of artillery fire, which swept 'the wood as a tropical storm sweeps the leaves from the trees of a forest.'[47]

The senior officials of the two battalions met to discuss a course of action. They decided to pull back their men in the wood and organize the 200 yards of captured trench for defence while holding on to the advanced line in hope that the requested reinforcements would be forthcoming.

The assault on Kitchener's Wood was still in progress when the 2nd and 3rd Battalions (1st Brigade) reported to General Turner. While sending the 3rd Battalion to take up a position 300 yards south of Mouse Trap Farm, Turner directed Lt.-Col. D. Watson to move his 2nd Battalion forward and assist in the counter-attack. Watson arrived at Juliet Farm shortly after 3 AM and, following a meeting there with Leckie, agreed to storm the German stronghold at the south-west corner of the wood.[48] He sent No. 1 Company to attack the German position, No. 2 Company to dig in on the 16th Battalion's right and No. 3 Company to occupy Oblong Farm to the left of the 10th Battalion.

As dawn approached the men of No. 1 Company crept silently forward but at 200 yards the mist suddenly lifted and they were spotted by German machine-gunners who opened fire. With little protection to hide behind the company was cut to ribbons and, of the dozen or so who managed to drag themselves back, nearly all were wounded. Although unproductive and costly, the attack had created a diversion sufficient to allow No. 3 Company to take Oblong Farm and mount a machine-gun behind a nearby hedge.

The failure of the attack raised fears that the Canadians beyond the wood might be cut off. Therefore, after another consultation between the officers on the spot, orders went out to evacuate the forward position. As the horses had not yet arrived a crew of engineers put the guns out of commission.

The coming of light revealed the enemy's grisly work of the night before. Hundreds of dead and wounded lay upon the open field, piled on one another or at intervals so close that it would have been almost impossible to walk through the area without stepping on a body. Groans could be heard and some of the bodies moved or twitched but in the face of German fire rescue attempts had to be abandoned.

The first Canadian attack of the war had failed with terrible losses. Later, when the troops acquired experience, they would learn to attack in open formation, preserve momentum by reinforcing the points of success, consolidate in stages, maintain a reserve against the unforeseen and bring stores with them in the third or fourth wave. But all of this was unknown to them at the time and they paid a high price for their ignorance.

To fill the 500-yard gap between the right of the 2nd Battalion and the St. Julien garrison, Turner sent up two companies of the 3rd Battalion. Prior to this he telephoned Second Brigade Headquarters and urgently requested help on the grounds that the enemy was in strength at Keerselaere and north of it.[49] Currie at once ordered the 7th Battalion (less one company) about Locality 'C' to march westward and extend the right flank of the St. Julien garrison to the end of the Gravenstafel Ridge. By 5.30 AM a continuous line existed from Oblong Farm to the crossroads east of Keerselaere.

But north of Keerselaere, for a distance of nearly a mile, the Allied flank still lay open. The next defended area was the new apex of the salient where the 13th and a small group of Zouaves lined the ditch along the Poelcappelle road. For McCuaig and his dwindling band the situation remained desperate. The Germans, apart from enjoying an overwhelming superiority in guns and numbers, had plenty of flares and, being able to command light at their pleasure, kept up the pressure all night. They rained shells on the trenches below and twice followed up with grenades and bayonet. Bleeding and exhausted though they were, McCuaig's men drove back both attacks after inflicting severe losses. In spite of a limited stock of ammunition the defenders replied each time with a veritable storm of rifle fire as they were determined to hide their numerical weakness from the enemy.

In the meantime McCuaig received a message from Loomis directing him to use his own judgment as to his dispositions. Thereupon McCuaig held consultations with the company commanders, Captains Jamieson and Clark-Kennedy, as a result of which he decided that if reinforcements failed to arrive before dawn he would evacuate the line of the road and occupy a new position about 300 yards in rear of and parallel to it. The new trench would shorten the front and provide a better field of fire than the old one. Thus McCuaig instructed Captain Jamieson to get his men to work on the new line.

Shortly before dawn, as no help had arrived, McCuaig ordered that the switch be made. Lieutenant Ross' machine-gun unit and Corporal McFarlane, with a dozen men, kept up a brisk fire to cover the movement, then retired successfully. This had barely been accomplished when, to the delight of the weary troops, the reinforcements appeared. Those consisted of B Company[50] (Captain F. W. Tomlinson) of the 2nd Battalion of the Buffs and two platoons (Captain C. J. Smith) of No. 3 Company of the 13th Battalion which, until a few hours ago, had formed part of the St. Julien garrison. The mixed force was led by Major V. C. Buchanan, who, as a result of Norsworthy's death, was now second in command of the regiment. On arrival Buchanan assumed control of the operations.

As the available forces were not sufficient for a counter-attack it was decided that McCuaig, with the remains of his own company and part of the Buffs, should reoccupy the trench just abandoned. Small parties filed off quietly in the dim light and, as hoped, the movement was completed without the enemy's knowledge.[51]

During the night Divisional Headquarters hurriedly improvised a second counter-attack, to be carried out by such forces as were available. At 1.05 AM General Alderson, having just met with General Plumer, ordered Colonel Geddes to push forward from St. Jean and link up with the Canadians at Kitchener's Wood and, if possible, with the right of Putz's battalions.[52] To ensure the safety of the British flank, Alderson sent the remaining two battalions of the 1st Brigade, the 1st and the 4th, to take up a position east of the canal.[53]

Warned that haste was essential, Geddes, handicapped by lack of staff, was not able to get his detachment under way before daybreak. He planned to close the gap by establishing two edges and gradually extending to the centre. The 2nd Buffs (less one company loaned to the 13th Battalion) were to join up with the flank of the 3rd Canadian Brigade and then prolong their left. The 3rd Middlesex (less two companies sent to guard the Brielen bridge over the Yser Canal) was to find the French and, having done so, deploy to the right to gain touch with the Buffs. The reserve battalion, the 5th King's Own, was to move forward in the centre. Left uncommitted was the 1st York and Lancaster, which was to follow the King's Own.

From Wieltje the Buffs advanced northward over open, practically level ground, and, passing west of Mouse Trap Farm, came under furious machine-gun fire. After losing two officers and 80 men they sought cover in some old trenches beyond the farm where their flanks eventually established contact with men of the 14th Canadian Battalion. The other unit, the 3rd Middlesex, in the course of moving forward

90

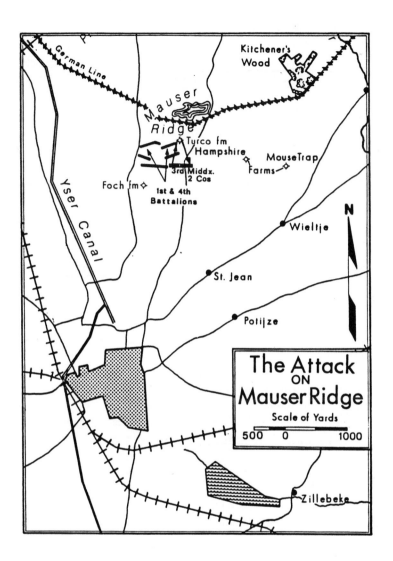

Kitchener's
Wood

M a u s e r

Ridge

Turco fm
Hampshire
MouseTrap
Farms

3rd Middx.
2 Cos

Foch fm

1st & 4th
Battalions

German Line

Yser Canal

Wieltje

St. Jean

Potijze

N

The Attack
ON
Mauser Ridge
Scale of Yards
500   0   1000

Zillebeke

between Hill Top and Pilckem, was surprised when its left found the 1st and 4th Canadian Battalions. It does not appear that Geddes had been informed of the intended movements of these two Canadian battalions.

The Canadians, the 1st Battalion under Lt.-Col. F.W. Hill and the 4th Battalion under Lt.-Col. A.P. Birchall, crossed the canal opposite Brielen and began their forward movement shortly after 3 AM. The Brigade Commander, Brig.-Gen. Mercer, received orders at 4.15 AM to co-operate in a French counter-attack against Pilckem, timed to start at 5 AM.[54] The plan was for the Canadians to deliver a thrust on the east side of the Ypres-Pilckem road while two French battalions of the 45th Division attacked north-east from the Yser Canal.[55] At Mercer's request the Middlesex joined in the counter-attack.

Slightly behind the crest of Hill Top Ridge the Canadians lined up in their formation with the 4th Battalion in the lead. Their first objective was to seize Mauser Ridge, a low hill some 1500 yards to the north. As the sun rose the Canadians could clearly see the Germans wiring their position across the valley. Everything was ready at the appointed hour but the French were nowhere in sight. At 5.25 AM Birchall, assuming that the French movement on his left was hidden by intervening trees and hedges, gave the order to advance.

The ground between was even, gently rolling countryside, offering little cover. Only eight light field guns and eight 4.5-inch howitzers were available to support the attack. These guns were incapable of bringing down anything like the kind of fire power needed to neutralize the defenders.

Marching in perfect order the infantry lines passed Foch's Farm where the supper lay untouched on the kitchen table and cows lowed for someone to milk their swollen udders. The moment they breasted Hill Top Ridge and began to descend the reverse slope the Germans opened up, supplementing rifle and machine-gun fire with an intense and well directed artillery barrage. As the bombs struck home men

92

crumbled in a hail of shrapnel or were tossed into the air by the blast of high explosive shells. Major Kelley of the 4th was hit and went down but he was never seen again. With men and officers falling at every step the advance continued, reaching a row of pollard willows, which marked the bottom of the valley. Here the Canadians were pinned to the ground by fierce enfilading fire from a spur of Mauser Ridge (southeast of Boesinghe), which the French had erroneously reported as still being in their hands.

On the right the two Middlesex companies steadily kept pace, advancing across the valley and up the slope ahead, to a cut bank within 400 yards of the nearest Germans. Reserve companies of the 1st Battalion were sent into action, extending the Canadian right and permitting the Middlesex to push on another 100 yards to occupy Turco Farm. However the Middlesex were shelled out by Canadian gunners who were unaware they had entered the farm.

The British advance was the high-water mark of the early morning's fighting. There were many casualties, especially in Canadian ranks. Among the first killed was Captain C.D. Brant, descendant of the line of fearless Mohawk chiefs who had fought on the side of Britain during the American Revolution and the War of 1812.

While the attack was in progress Mercer received an assuring message from Colonel Mordacq, who was in charge of the French operations, that three and a half battalions of Zouaves were operating east of the canal with two more about to cross.[56] But by 8.30 AM there was still no sign of any such action. Thus Mercer sent orders to his 1st and 4th Battalions to dig in, but to advance again if the French did so.[57]

The forward movement of Geddes' and Mercer's troops meant that a fairly continuous line had been established from Keerselaere to within 1200 yards of the canal. There was every hope that before long this gap too would be filled. Still, the situation as a whole remained critical. The seventeen and a half Canadian-British battalions in the first and second lines, rushed up at utmost speed during the night or early morning, were weary, hungry, forced to fight from unprepared positions frequently located on lower ground, in many cases sadly reduced in numbers and supported only by the artillery of a division. These faced 42 German battalions, which enjoyed a preponderance of at least five to one in divisional guns and an even greater superiority in heavy artillery.

The lull in German activity following the break-in, caused to a large extent by the tenacious resistance of scattered parties of Canadians, had enabled Alderson to establish a very sketchy and precarious line. Throughout the day on the 23rd the Germans showed the same disinclination to press home their advantage. They contented themselves with a few isolated attacks against the improvised flank and with slightly improving their position opposite the French on the west bank of the canal. And their guns, frequently using tear-gas shells, continued to bombard the whole area, in particular the apex of the front of the Canadian Division. The German Command was under the impression that by constricting the salient the Allies would evacuate it. Given further breathing space the British struggled to remove the threat of a German advance down to Ypres by sealing the gap on their left flank.

No further major action or movement occurred on the morning of the 23rd. At the end of the flank the 1st and 4th Battalions remained where they had entrenched and a request was made to the French to fill the opening on the left of these units.[1] The 2nd Zouaves moved up to Pilckem road and established contact with the Canadians shortly after midday.[2] Thus the line from Keerselaere to the canal was completed. Throughout much of the day Mercer's men, as well as the Middlesex, were subjected to a barrage of tear-gas bombs, causing them to cough violently and irritating their eyes to a point where they were unable to see. The effects were only temporary and passed when the shelling ceased.

Of more immediate danger were the Allied units on the left of the original line. As already noted McCuaig, with the arrival of reinforcements, had reoccupied the front trench. Shortly afterwards a number of figures, apparently wearing French uniforms but indistinct in the early morning light, appeared in rear of the Algerian trenches, crying out, 'We are the French.' McCuaig, Tomlinson of the Buffs and a French officer were standing at a point where the trenches crossed the road. They suspected a ruse and, failing to receive satisfactory answers to their queries, ordered their troops to open fire. While the imposters scrambled for cover, their comrades replied in kind.

The incident marked the beginning of fresh fighting. German shelling intensified and, directed by aeroplanes, was extremely accurate. The price of trying to hold the barrier along the road became too costly and at 9 AM McCuaig decided to abandon it and retire into the trench-line proper. This helped somewhat but as soon as the Germans got behind McCuaig they were able to pour rifle fire on his position from three sides. The fire from the rear was especially effective as the trenches were badly battered and the hastily constructed parados provided little protection.[3] In an effort to reduce the enfilading fire, Lieutenant Ross set up two machine-gun posts. One, being rather exposed, was silenced but the other succeeded in neutralizing the most bothersome of the opposing trenches. This partial protection from enfilading fire was welcomed but as the day wore on things did not augur well for the men of the 13th and their allies. The shelling had not abated and they were short of food and water and dangerously low on ammunition. Communication with the rear remained completely cut while communication between companies themselves was extremely difficult. Messages were carried by volunteer runners who had to duck and worm their way through sniper and artillery fire.

Throughout the night and during the morning of the 23rd reinforcing battalions from the reserves of British divisions to the south had been hurrying into the Canadian sector. If the aim had been to form a defensible line along the Canadian flank this might have been achieved without excessive loss. However, the French would settle for nothing less than restoration of the original front.

Thus far they had not contributed anything toward that end. They were highly apologetic about their non-appearance on each of the two occasions. On the morning of the 23rd they made the usual extravagant promises that their counter-attack would take place in the afternoon when the new batteries arrived to replace the guns lost in the gas attack.

Anxiety over conditions on the French front was augmented by reports suggesting that the Germans were preparing to launch an attack from Kitchener's Wood toward St. Julien. Columns of motor lorries were seen moving southwards, bringing fresh troops to reinforce the line north of Kitchener's Wood to beyond Keerselaere. After penetrating into Keerselaere the Germans, as related already, had forced the left of the 13th Battalion and a company of Buffs to abandon a redoubt on the road at 9 AM. Judging the enemy to be in great strength Loomis warned Turner at 10.50 AM that he would soon have to withdraw his exposed left from the original line into the trenches at St. Julien. If, on the other hand, he received support he would be in a position to counterattack in order to drive the Germans west of the St. Julien-Poelcappelle road.[4] Accordingly he dispatched Captain Clark-Kennedy, who had returned from the 13th Battalion's front, to explain the situation personally to General Turner.[5]

By now aerial observations confirmed earlier reports that the Germans were massing north of Kitchener's Wood, very near the Canadian flank. To the west they had dug in and wired a strong position on Mauser ridge in front of Langemarck-Pilckem ridge and were constructing a second line between the north end of Kitchener's Wood and Pilckem. It was apparent that they could not be driven back without a major effort and this, for the moment, was out of the question. Alderson had already dispersed the Divisional reserve and neither the 2nd nor 3rd Brigades had any troops to spare. All that remained of the V Corps reserve were a few battalions borrowed from the 27th and 28th Divisions. The Second Army had no reserves left, except the 13 Brigade, currently resting south of Vlamertinghe after its ordeal at Hill 60.

Clark-Kennedy was ushered into Turner's office on reaching 3rd Brigade Headquarters. He was convinced that something quickly had to be done for, failing a strong counter-attack, retirement was inevitable. Turner then discussed the matter with Divisional Headquarters by telephone. He received a sympathetic hearing but little else. At 11.03 AM Division Headquarters replied, suggesting that the 13th Battalion fall back to support trenches and that the 7th cover the gap between the St. Julien defenders and the left of the 15th. Turner's only consolation was that he was promised two companies of the 9th Royal Scots (27th Division).[6] No sooner had these arrived than they were ordered back in order to participate in the combined Anglo-French attack further west. Loomis was left to defend his front as best he could.

With the view to blunt an anticipated south-east thrust behind his line, Turner ordered the reserve units of the 15th Battalion to take a position in rear of the 13th. Between the 15th Battalion's supports and St. Julien, the 7th (less one company left as a garrison for Locality C) occupied a hill, at the foot of which was the village of Keerselaere.[7] The 7th Battalion had only recently moved up and in the afternoon it received an order to dig and fortify a new trench line, under cover of darkness. The commander of the 7th, Lt.-Col. W.F.R. Hart-McHarg, was a prominent criminal lawyer and a rifleman of international fame. The question confronting him was whether the new line should be dug in the open ground, where the battalion then lay, or down at the foot of the hill. Major Odlum, second in command, observed that he had already reconnoitred the area and in his judgment 'our existing position on the high ground was the right one and that if we went down to a forward position at the foot of the slope our communications would be very much exposed and endangered.'[8] Hart-McHarg was inclined to agree but he wanted to go out and see for himself.[9]

Accordingly, Hart-McHarg, accompanied by Odlum and

Lieutenant D.M. Matheson of the Engineers, proceeded cautiously down the hill to the wrecked houses and shattered walls of the village. As they looked through a window in the rear of one of the ruins they were amazed to see masses of Germans lined up behind hedges scarcely a hundred yards away, watching them intently.[10] All three turned and ran, Matheson veering off to the left to take shelter in a ditch while the other two struck straight up the hill. The instant they cleared the ruins they were followed by a burst of rapid fire. Both threw themselves to the ground. Odlum, by luck, jumped into a small shell hole directly in front and a moment later Hart-McHarg rolled on top of him, exclaiming 'I don't want to get hit again.' 'Get what again?' Odlum asked. 'I'm shot,' he replied. 'Where?' 'Through the stomach, oh my God.'[11] He had been struck from behind, through the left thigh, the bullet penetrating his stomach.[12]

Odlum slid out from under his stricken comrade and did what he could to comfort him. The colonel was in great pain and would not let Odlum tend to his wound, begging him to get the doctor. 'Frankly, I did not want to,' Odlum said afterwards. 'I felt much safer where I was and I had it in my mind to remain in the shell hole until ... darkness when we could get out safely. But his suffering was too much for me....'[13] Awaiting his opportunity Odlum made a zig zag dash up the remainder of the hill, the Germans firing at him as he went. He found Captain George Gibson, the battalion medical officer, and explained to him what had happened.[14] Gibson volunteered to go out at once, and, with Sergeant J. Dryden, made his way down to the shell hole where Hart-McHarg lay. Between them they moved the colonel to a nearby ditch—where Matheson had taken cover—and there dressed his wound. They remained with him until after dark when the stretcher-bearers arrived and carried him to a little ruined farmhouse, which served as battalion headquarters.[15]

A robust man might have survived the wound but the 46-year-old Hart-McHarg had been in frail health for some years and he knew he was dying. During the night he found comfort in gently clasping the hand of Odlum who, when duty permitted, sat by his side. There were many things he wanted to say but he had great difficulty in speaking. Toward midnight an ambulance arrived and conveyed the sinking colonel to Poperinghe where he died the next day.[16] Cool, daring and judicious, with enormous natural ability and a dominating personality, he would undoubtedly have risen to high command in the Canadian Army had he lived. To perpetuate his memory a tablet in bronze, erected by his comrades, was unveiled in Christ Church, Vancouver, on 13, November 1921. Major Odlum succeeded to the command of the 7th Battalion.

The situation in the Ypres salient was under careful scrutiny at British General Headquarters where the piecemeal reports had trickled in during the night of 22-23 April. Hardly an hour passed when Sir John did not revile the French for their headlong flight. 'Although the gas no doubt had something to do with the panic,' Sir John later wrote to Lord Kitchener, 'this would never have happened if the French had not weakened their line a good deal too much.'[17] He had in earlier conversations with both Joffre and Foch expressed misgivings about the quality of the French units that covered the left of the British Army in the salient. The French leaders made no effort to replace or strengthen these second rate troops, perhaps because they hoped to induce the British to take over that section of the line.

Since August, the 63-year-old French had faced more than his share of military crises, which all too frequently he had mishandled. His pre-1914 reputation was based almost exclusively on his leadership of the cavalry in the South African War, especially in the operation around Colesberg and in the relief of the siege of Kimberley. A short, thickly-built man with a bushy moustache, he was personally fearless of danger and could inspire his men as few commanders could. His assets, however, could not begin to compensate for his liabilities. He had an unstable personality, veering sharply from optimism to gloom, from confidence to indecision. He was unimaginative, inexperienced in handling large bodies of men and ignorant of the tactical and strategic principles of modern warfare. His shortcomings were repeatedly evident not only during the war of movement but also after the deadlock set in. French was the classic example of a man who had risen above the level of his competence.

It was clear to French that the German action on 22 April had gravely imperilled his front. According to all rules of warfare the only sensible thing was to fall back with all haste in order to straighten the line. On the morning of the 23rd Sir John motored to Cassel to impress this option upon Foch.

As Joffre's deputy, Foch had control of the northern Front and was charged with the responsibility of co-ordinating the efforts of the French, British and Belgians. On hearing the news of the German break-in, he directed General Putz to make sure of holding the line now occupied and to organize a counter-attack to regain the lost ground. For this he ordered the Tenth Army to send the 153rd Division to General Putz, warning that more troops might be required.[18]

If we are to understand Foch's behaviour at this time, an examination of his character and military background would be useful. First as instructor and then as commandant of the Ecole Supérieure de la guerre, Foch had played a key role in shaping the military philosophy of the French Army prior to the First World War.[19] In a series of lectures subsequently published as *Principes de la guerre* (1903) and *Conduite de la guerre* (1904), Foch fascinated his audiences by expounding a doctrine that stressed the transcendence of the moral factors over the material. He contended that the basic formula for victory was Napoleonic audacity, seeking out battle immediately and attacking without thought of cost or possibility of tactical manoeuvre. His teachings permeated the upper levels of the French Army, which incorporated into the new Field Regulations in 1913 the idea of *l'offensive à outrance*—attack to the absolute limit. Included in the Field Regulations was the following paragraph:

> Battles are above all else struggles of morale. Defeat is inevitable as soon as the hope of victory ceases. Success comes not to him who has suffered least, but to him who has the strongest will and the highest morale.

Nowhere in the manual is there any emphasis on supplies, fire-power or defensive action. Even after the opening months of the war, in which their armies had suffered shattering defeats, the French military leaders refused to acknowledge they had been wrong to assume that attacking infantry required essentially determination in order to win.

Now 64, Foch was still remarkably fit and alert, in both body and mind. He was a sincere, engaging little man and, being typically French, was fond of gesticulating to emphasize a point. His unshakeable character and faith in his beliefs made it difficult for anyone in his company to hold firm to contrary opinions. His tactical limitations were at least partially offset by the fact that he looked like a general and possessed many of the qualities of a true leader. He radiated strength, authority and confidence and always stood ready to accept responsibility whatever the circumstances.

Of all the French generals, Foch alone enjoyed a harmonious working relationship with the choleric Sir John. He understood Sir John's state of mind and in conversation with him was reassuring, tactful and deferential. However strange and unreasonable Sir John's proposition might be, Foch never countered with a refusal or criticism. He would begin by outlining the merits of the proposal and then gently bring Sir John around, step-by-step, often leading him to accept his own views. In difficult times Foch behaved with such firmness and conviction that Sir John, troubled and anxious at the start, would leave the interview comforted and confident.

The meeting on 23 April ended like most of the previous ones with Foch getting his way. There is no known record of the exchanges but the results show that Sir John committed himself to a course of action exactly opposite to that which he had proposed. Foch assured the Field Marshal that he intended to regain the ground lost by the 45th and 87th Divisions. To that end he had ordered up large reinforcements and already two battalions and three batteries had reported to General Putz. The British Commander agreed to co-operate in the attack but reserved the right to withdraw his troops from the threatened salient if the French position was not soon re-established.

The contracted salient was a potential death-trap. The improvised British flank was very fragile, with practically no supports, and at any moment it was apt to be overwhelmed by vastly superior enemy forces. Compounding Sir John's fears was the possibility that a renewed thrust by the German XXIIIrd Reserve Corps across the canal near Steenstraat might rupture the line between the Belgians and the French. The Field Marshal's concerns were well founded.

Impressed by the progress of his army during the first day's fighting, the Duke of Albrecht believed that the original objective, the Yser Canal, might now be substantially broadened. Thus he issued instructions in the early hours of the 23rd for the attack to continue in the direction of Poperinghe. The XXIIIrd Reserve Corps was to advance west of the canal to the line Boesinghe-Pyegaale (in Belgian hands, 2000 yards north-west of Steenstraat), while the XXVIth Reserve Corps, its right wing along the canal, swept southwards with the purpose of smashing the Canadian flank and sweeping away the British forces in front of the XXVIIth Reserve Corps.

The assault of the XXIIIrd Reserve against the French and Belgians encountered extraordinary difficulties and failed to realize any of its objectives. On the other hand the vigorous Canadian counter-attacks in the early morning left the

XXVIth Reserve Corps in no condition to execute the movement ordered. Later in the day the German High Command intervened and informed Albrecht 'that Poperinghe did not primarily enter the question at all as an objective and that for the present it was strictly a matter of cutting off the Ypres salient.'[20]

Backed at his advanced headquarters, located at Hazebrouck, French instructed Smith-Dorrien to assist General Putz's advance, making available the infantry of the 50th Division and subsequently the entire Cavalry Corps. Around 1 PM the 1st Cavalry Division arrived in the Ypres area and with it the 13th Infantry Brigade, released from Army reserve and now at the disposal of General Alderson.

At 1.20 PM General Quiquandon, commanding the 45th Algerian, ordered the 90th Brigade (Colonel Mordacq) to advance northward between Boesinghe and the Ypres-Pilckem road.[21] The attack was set for 3 PM. As zero hour approached and the French appeared to be doing nothing, Smith-Dorrien grew anxious lest a delay enable the Germans to further fortify their position. Following consultations with General Plumer, Smith-Dorrien became convinced that if an attack was to take place at all it must be made immediately. At 2.30 PM he issued orders to the V Corps for a general attack between Kitchener's Wood and Yser Canal.

According to the plan the 13th Brigade, led by Brig.-Gen. R. Wanless O'Gowan, was to cross the Brielen bridge, form up and move forward toward Pilckem with its right on the Pilckem-Ypres road. The effort on the east side of the road was entrusted to the fresh battalions (2nd East Yorkshire, 5th King's Own, 1st York and Lancaster) of Geddes' Detachment and two battalions (2nd Duke of Cornwall's LI and 9th Royal Scots) of the 27th Division. The remaining units of Geddes' Detachment, along with the 1st and 4th Canadian Battalions, were to provide what assistance they could as the operation developed. After the capture of Pilckem the attack was to continue until the old French line was restored.[22]

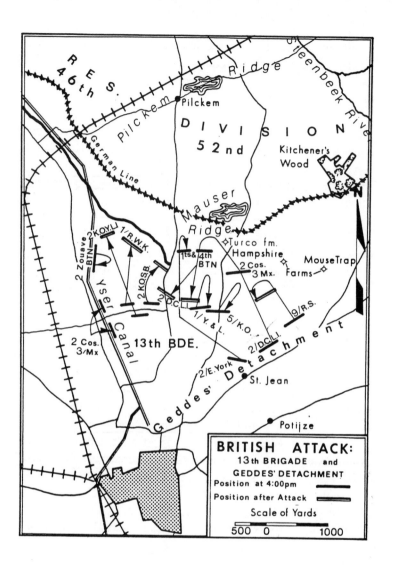

R E S.
46th

Pilckem Ridge

Pilckem

Greenbeek Riv.

D I V I S I O N
52nd

German Line

Kitchener's
Wood

N

Mauser
Ridge

2 KOYLI   1/R.W.K.

2 Zouave BTN

1ts & 4th
BTN

Turco fm.
Hampshire

MouseTrap
Farms

2 Cos.
3 Mx.

2 KOSB

Yser Canal

2/D.C.Li.

1/Y. & L.

5/K.O.

9/R.S.

2/D.C.Li.

2 Cos.
3/Mx.

13th BDE.

Geddes' Detachment

2/E. York

St. Jean

Potijze

BRITISH ATTACK:
13th BRIGADE and
GEDDES' DETACHMENT
Position at 4:00pm
Position after Attack
Scale of Yards
500   0   1000

Because General Quiquandon mistakenly believed that the British objective was Langemarck, he ordered the 90th Brigade to attack in an area subsequently allotted to Wanless O'Gowan's 13th Brigade. General Alderson apparently did not receive the French operation order in time to change his own. Thus when the men of the 13th, having followed a circuitous route, swung too far north, they entered the French zone and found the roads occupied by Algerian troops.[23] After the swearing had stopped and the confusion sorted out it was decided on the spot to postpone the Allied push until 4.25 PM.

The attack to which the Second Army was committed was doomed to fail before it started. Like the one in the morning it was directed against Mauser Ridge. The infantry had to advance in broad daylight over ground that was very open, broken only by a few widely scattered hedges, and which sloped gently up, over a distance of about half a mile, to the enemy's first line. The 13th Brigade was physically tired and its numbers reduced by the heavy fighting at Hill 60. And the units previously uncommitted had, of course, not seen any action but they had been on their feet for almost 24 hours. Since the operation was organized in haste there was a lack of preparation and no reconnaissance even to determine the enemy's exact location. On top of all this the infantry assault was launched without the customary artillery support. The gunners, scattered as they were and coming under different commands, were not informed of the change in the time of the attack. They opened fire at 2.45 PM and after a brief period stopped. When the assault actually got under way a shortage of ammunition prevented another preliminary bombardment.

The left of the attack was formed by the 13th Brigade. In the centre, troops of Geddes' Detachment passed through ground that the 1st and 4th Canadian Battalions and the 3rd Middlesex had been holding since early morning. On the right were the two battalions of the 27th Division under Lt.-

Col. H.D. Tuson. Each battalion was allotted 500 yards of front and was organized in five or six lines at wide intervals. Tuson's Duke of Cornwall and Royal Scots were sent in half an hour after the general advance began at 4.25 PM.

Alerted by the artillery barrage, the Germans opened fire as soon as the leading waves came into their view. In the clear light, with every man distinctly visible, German machine-gunners reaped a bountiful harvest. British officers took an unusually high proportion of the casualties and, as little information came back, the direction of the battle broke down.

The 13th Brigade had advanced some 500 yards from the Brielen bridge when it established contact with the French right on the canal. A sudden rush by a battalion of Zouaves, whose zero hour had been set at 5 PM, cut across the front of the 13th, temporarily halting the 1st Royal West Kent and the 2nd King's Own Scottish Borders and crowding them to the right. The two British battalions resumed their progress when the Zouaves, following a feeble effort, withdrew. Along the canal where the ground was a little more enclosed, some units of the 13th worked their way up the slope and got as far as the enemy outpost line before being brought to a standstill.

Next, in the centre, Geddes' men came under annihilating fire the instant they rose from the ground. The first two lines were practically cut down to a man but the dust and smoke offered partial protection to those that followed and they slowly crept forward. Some parties closed to about 100 yards of the enemy's main position while one small detachment of East Yorkshires fought to within 30 yards.

Shaking off their previous losses and exertions the 1st and 4th Canadian Battalions and the Middlesex joined in the attack. They advanced over the same ground as they had in the morning and the results were no different. German machine-guns and shrapnel tore large gaps in their already depleted ranks. The 4th Battalion came under particularly devastating fire and for a moment wavered. Its commander Lt.-Col. Birchall, conspicuous on account of his great height and the light cane he carried, coolly rallied it and passed the order to charge. He fell, pierced by three bullets, but his men, mad with rage, sprang forward and pushed home the attack in the face of direct frontal fire. They stormed one of the enemy's outer redoubt and after a hand-to-hand struggle captured it. But they could advance no further and once again had to dig in.

On the far right the Royal Scots and the Duke of Cornwall made a little progress. The former found German fire so intense that they were compelled to halt short of Hampshire Farm. The latter did slightly better, reoccupying Turco Farm.

With the approach of darkness all movements came to an end. Casualties had been heavy, running between 200 and 400 in most of the battalions. The morning and afternoon attacks had accounted for the loss of 404 all ranks in the 1st Canadian Battalion and 454 in the 4th Battalion, including the CO who was killed. In paying a heavy price these men of the 1st Brigade had acquitted themselves magnificently. Looking back across the years a survivor of the 4th Battalion declared:

> It was a glorious day for the Canadians because these men had had practically no training. But was I ever proud of them. If they'd have been trained for ten years they couldn't have acted better. To think of those kids that had been pulled from all over the country and the way they behaved! In a murderous fire like that! I never felt so proud of a bunch of boys in my life.[24]

The British action at Mauser Ridge had the effect of stopping any further German advance in this quarter but at a cost that was unjustifiable. The verdict of the British Official History was that, given the openness of the country, the ground gained could have been secured by a night advance, probably with few or no casualties.[25]

The evening of 23 April was cloudy, without a moon, and around 9.30 PM the British leaders ordered their men to fall back to a new line in rear of the high-water mark of the attack, some 600 yards south of the enemy. Organization of this position proceeded only with great difficulty. The units were mixed up and there was such confusion that daylight found some survivors digging in facing the wrong way.[26] The ground was completely waterlogged so that it was impossible to dig deep trenches. The men spent a miserable night though they were undisturbed by the Germans. Some rations in the nature of bread and bacon were brought up but the distribution was so haphazard that many men remained 24 hours without food.

French assistance on the west side of the canal, which Foch had promised, did not amount to much. As noted earlier the Zouaves made a brief appearance on the battlefield before scurrying back to the safety of their own line. During the day Foch went to see Putz on two occasions to urge him to greater efforts. He received no special assurances. Putz saw no point in sending out thoroughly demoralized troops across bullet-swept ground and, being of stronger fibre than Sir John, was less susceptible to pressure.

It would have been better if Foch and his commanders had arrived at a common policy before making commitments that they could not hope to meet. As it was they forced the Canadians and the British into hurriedly improvised operations and left them in the lurch, ensuring defeat and many more casualties than would otherwise have been the case. Lt.-Col. Gordon Hall, GSO2 of the Canadian Division, remarked bitterly:

> If we had only ourselves to consider we might have organized one proper counter-attack with adequate numbers as soon as they were available. Fewer troops would have been

required; we could not have suffered more heavily; we would not have had our troops mixed up and disorganized; and at least we might have been able to form a decent flank and avoid the disastrous break at the apex on the 24th. All due to Foch and his Divisional Commanders, whose idea seemed to be that the British must sacrifice themselves in holding on, till they themselves were quite ready to take on the job in a big way with adequate troops and make a spectacular exhibition of it. [27]

The Canadians showed the same dogged determination in their defensive operations as in their counter-attacks. All day shells rained on St. Julien and the covering trenches, ceasing only when an attack was imminent. On four occasions the Germans came out of their trenches and each time they were driven back by rifle and machine-gun fire. But German artillery continued to take a heavy toll and Loomis concluded that he must retrench after dark as Alderson had suggested. Under the plan worked out, the 7th Battalion would be extended so as to link it with the St. Julien garrison and the left of the 15th Battalion in the old line. [28]

At the apex of the front, opposite Poelcappelle, the position of the 13th Battalion and its allies was progressively deteriorating. Around 5 PM Captain Clark-Kennedy returned to the firing line after meetings with Loomis and Turner. He brought with him orders from Brigade Headquarters instructing Major Buchanan to retire to a new line running to the rear from the point where his present front joined with that of the next battalion, the 15th. Before acting on these instruction Buchanan passed the word to bury the dead and commence the removal of the wounded.

The retirement had barely begun when the Germans, sensing the move, attacked from three sides. The Allies were in danger of being overwhelmed as they had exhausted their supply of grenades and were loaded down with large numbers of wounded. That this did not occur was due to the gallant

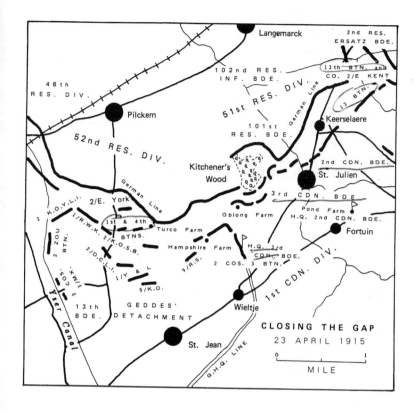

CLOSING THE GAP
23 APRIL 1915

work of a small rear guard under the command of Lieutenant C.B. Pitblado and supported by Lieutenant J.G. Ross with two machine-guns. As it was, the German attacks were beaten off and the withdrawl continued. Arriving to the position designated by General Turner, the Buffs and the men of the 13th laid down the wounded and began to dig in. The Germans made no further move that night, allowing the exhausted survivors to rest and slake their thirst.[29]

By the end of the 23rd the position of the Canadian flank was slightly better off than on the previous day. However, the improvement had been achieved at the expense of heavy casualties and of having to throw into the fight every battalion in divisional and corps reserve and the two brigades of the Second Army reserve, the 13th and the 1st Canadian. Although little ground had been regained, a continuous though tenuous line had been established, from the apex of the 3rd Canadian Brigade to South Zwaanhof Farm, beside the canal where a battalion of the 13th Brigade joined with the French right flank. Apart from a few hundred Zouaves along the canal bank there were no French troops on the east side and the safety of the British divisions in the salient was still very much in doubt.

Late reports from the west side of the canal were mixed, giving rise first to hope and then to apprehension. The Belgians not only maintained their front intact near Steenstraat but the arrival of fresh units permitted them to reinforce the junction with the French left. General Quiquandon had the situation near Boesinghe in hand and he was confident of being able to hold the line of the canal. On the other hand the Germans remained in possession of the bridgeheads at Het Sas and Steenstraat and the ground between, and around 1.30 AM on 24 April captured Lizerne, menacing the French position on the west bank.[30]

To General Headquarters it appeared that the Germans were delaying their advance against the new British flank in order to concentrate their efforts on making a breach between the French and the Belgians and sweeping the former away. On the morning of the 24th Sir John directed Smith-Dorrien not to place much reliance on the French and to secure his left as soon as his dispositions would permit it. He added that vigorous action east of the canal was the best means of checking the enemy's advance westward through General Putz's troops.[31] One cannot help but question the Field Marshall's decision given the circumstances—the previous day's losses, the confused and demoralized condition of many of the units, the extreme tactical vulnerability of the British position and the absence of any effective protection against the gas. However, as so often happened in the war, the Germans struck first.

Aerial reconnaissance made at dawn on the 24th detected the presence of 30 trains at Menin and seven at Ledeghem (ten miles east of Ypres) but no unusual German movements. The trains consisted of covered coaches and might have brought up reinforcements but they might also have been empty and intended for the evacuation of the wounded. As a precautionary move Smith-Dorrien warned units of his army, especially the II Corps, which was south of the V Corps and opposite Menin-Ledeghem, to be alert for any signs of an attack.

With the Germans free to select any of a number of options, the British High Command had no sure way of knowing where the next blow might descend. Suspecting the the enemy would attempt a thrust across the canal to split the Belgians and French at Steenstraat and Lizerne, Sir John had ordered the Second Army to initiate vigorous counter-measures. This action was in keeping with the Field Marshal's policy to disconcert or frustrate co-ordinated and synchronized undertakings by the enemy. Such attacks, even if costly and individually hopeless, were regarded as the best antidote to limit scope and reduce effectiveness. And so Sir John, in the belief that he was preserving his own position in the salient as well as gaining time until the French were ready for a big spectacular effort, pressed a series of ill-prepared attacks across open country against an enemy who was entrenched on higher ground and backed by superior firepower. As might be expected all were brought to a standstill with casualties far out of proportion to the ground gained.

Forestalled in his drive to capture Ypres by the counter-attacks of the 23rd, the Duke of Albrecht laid deliberate plans to roll up the Canadian line. The direction of the wind was favourable and the remainder of the gas cylinders could be used. The discharge, set for 4 AM on the 24th, was to be accompanied by a bombardment of T-STOFF shells to thicken the cloud and to increase its psychological effects and followed by a converging attack on the Canadian-held apex.

The assault would be led by the left wing of the XXVIth Reserve Corps, the 51st Reserve Division and the 2nd Reserve Ersatz Brigade, and supported by the Brigade Schmieden, a formation organized from battalions of the XXVIIth Reserve Corps. Next to the 2nd Reserve Ersatz was the 38th Landwehr forming the extreme right of the XXVIIth Reserve Corps. This corps would distract the British with shelling and local thrusts and subsequently join in the advance as the XXVIth swept southward. The purpose of the attack was to crush together the old and new Canadian lines, capture St. Julien, and by penetrating into the heart of the salient, force the abandonment of Ypres.

Simultaneously the XXIIIrd Reserve Corps (which had seized Lizerne at 1.30 AM) would continue its operations on the west side of the canal in order to capture the position Pypegaale-Zuydschoote-Boesinghe. Once this was accomplished the next objective was to circle southward to cut off the line of retreat at Vlamertinghe while the salient was being driven in. [1]

Along the Canadian front the men had worked through the night at preparing to meet a renewal of the enemy's attack that was expected at daylight. The infantry strengthened parapets, filled sandbags, built traverses and deepened the trenches. Telephone linemen repaired and extended communications. Transport parties brought up supplies, ammunition and even a few letters and parcels from Canada.

The line on both sides of the apex, from near Gravenstafel round to Kitchener's Wood, was manned by the equivalent of eight battalions. These faced no fewer than 24 German battalions. On the east side of the salient the 5th and 8th Battalions of the 2nd Brigade and the 15th Battalion were still in their old trenches. At the apex the line swung back sharply with a company of 2nd Buffs, the 13th and 7th Battalions carrying it to St. Julien. North of St. Julien No. 2 Company of the 15th and No. 2 Company of the 14th were augmented by the recent arrival of No. 4 Company of the 14th. From here the line was continued by half of the 3rd, the 16th and the 10th Battalions as far as the south-west corner of the wood.

In the early hours of the 24th the Germans, backed by gas shells, attempted to turn the Belgian flank from Lizerne. The Belgians gallantly held their ground and by extending their right south-west around Zuydschoote not only regained touch with the French but threatened to outflank the attackers. The French made two counter-attacks against Lizerne and, though they failed to enter the village, managed to close on three sides of it. On the other hand, their effort to recapture Het Sas miscarried.[2]

It was further south that some of the bitterest fighting of the war occurred. At 4 AM three red flares floated down from a German balloon hovering over Westroosebeke. A few moments later German artillery saturated Canadian trenches with a deluge of shells, scattering sandbags and killing sentries at watch on the firesteps. At the apex, men of the 15th and 8th Battalions noticed that something unusual was happening. A number of Germans appeared above their trenches, wearing grotesque helmets, something resembling a diver's headgear. Each held a hose from which began to flow a greenish yellow vapour. The chlorine, covering a 1200 yard front, was aimed directly at the junction of the 15th and 8th Battalions. Driven by a dawn breeze, the gas cloud, estimated to be fifteen feet high, came on rapidly like a greenish fog bank across no man's land. Canadian sentries sounded the alarm and hurried calls for artillery support brought prompt aid to the 8th Battalion. For the 15th Battalion on the left, however, no such help was forthcoming because the guns assigned to back the 3rd Infantry Brigade had been moved behind the GHQ Line and were out of range.[3]

There was no panic among the Canadians, partly because they had not been caught by surprise. Although effective

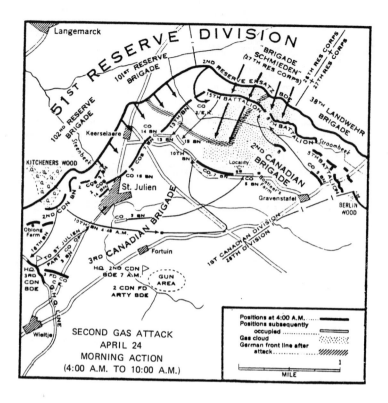

Langemarck

51ST RESERVE DIVISION

101ST RESERVE BRIGADE

102ND RESERVE BRIGADE

2ND RESERVE ERSATZ BDE

"BRIGADE SCHMIEDEN" (27TH RES CORPS)

26TH RES CORPS + 27TH RES CORPS

38TH LANDWEHR BRIGADE

Keerselaere

Steenbeek

KITCHENERS WOOD

CO 14 BN

13 BN

CO 1/E.K.

15TH BATTALION

15TH BN

11 BN

CO 7 BN

CO 10TH BN

CO 8 BN

Locality "C"

CO 7 BN

Boetleer's Farm

7TH BATTALION

2ND CANADIAN BRIGADE

5TH BATTALION

CO 8 BN

Stroombeek

St. Julien

CO 15 BN

CO 3 BN

CO 8 BN

Gravenstafel

BERLIN WOOD

2ND CDN BN

Oblong Farm

16TH BN

10TH BN 4.45 A.M.

TO ST JULIEN PART CO OF 3 BN

3RD CANADIAN BRIGADE

Fortuin

1ST CANADIAN DIVISION 28TH DIVISION

HQ 3RD CDN BDE

3 FD CO C.H.Q. LINE

HQ 2ND CDN BDE 7 A.M.

2 CDN FD ARTY BDE

GUN AREA

Wieltje

**SECOND GAS ATTACK
APRIL 24
MORNING ACTION
(4:00 A.M. TO 10:00 A.M.)**

Positions at 4:00 A.M. ....
Positions subsequently
  occupied ....
Gas cloud
German front line after
  attack............ ...//////////

1

MILE

means to resist gas attacks were not yet available,[4] they knew that breathing through a double handful of moist earth or a wet handkerchief afforded some measure of relief—indeed the 8th Battalion was provided with cotton bandoliers and buckets of water were stationed within easy reach. They also realized that it was best to remain in place.[5] The effort of running away, with the consequent heavier breathing, simply increased the poison in the lungs. Thus the Canadians faced the gas cloud, hoping that the blindness and searing pain would pass.

The deadly fumes enveloped the whole of the 15th Battalion's right company (No. 1) and much of the centre company (No. 3) as well as most of the 8th Battalion's left company (No. 1) and a small part of the centre company (No. 2).[6] In his account of the battle, Lt.-Col. H.H. Matthews wrote:

> It is impossible for me to give a real idea of the terror and horror spread among us all by this filthy loathsome pestilence. It was not, I think, the fear of death or anything supernatural but the great dread that we could not stand the fearful suffocating sensation sufficiently to be each in our proper places and able to resist to the uttermost the attack which we felt sure must follow....[7]

Coughing, choking and with eyes streaming, men held dampened cotton bandoliers or moistened handkerchiefs over their faces. Neither measure was of much value against the biting chlorine gas. Many were blinded and overcome, then tumbled to the bottom of the trenches where, gasping for air, they died in frightful agony. Those able to fight, reacting to the order that the line must be held at all costs, dragged themselves up onto the parapet and awaited the enemy.

Ten minutes after the gas had been released, the Germans scrambled out of their trenches wearing their respirators and with bayonets fixed. They were so confident that the chlorine had done their work that they advanced, not in open skirmishing order, but in heavy waves—one eyewitness even claimed that they were marching in column of fours.[8]

On the front of the 8th Battalion the centre and right that had escaped the gas, enfiladed the steady advancing grey figures with rifle and machine-gun fire, while the left, protected somewhat by the improvised gas masks and encouraged by the 2nd Field Artillery's accurate shrapnel barrage, poured a deadly fire into the approaching lines. As their Ross rifles jammed repeatedly under the stress of rapid fire the men, cursing, some even sobbing, in exasperation, used their boot heels or entrenching tool handles to try to pry back the stubborn bolts.[9] When rifle fire slackened the Canadians threw back the Germans with machine-gun bursts and bayonet thrusts. Many of the wounded sitting or lying at the bottom of the trenches loaded empty rifles and passed them up to their comrades on the firing step. Stricken by fire they had not expected, the attacking lines wavered, broke up, then stopped.

It was a different story for the 15th Battalion. No. 4 company on the left, outside the gassed area, could not provide aid for it was unable to see the front of the attack. Consequently the centre (No. 3) and right (No. 1) companies, which had received a full dose of the chlorine, were left to their own devices without either artillery support or enfilading fire. These soldiers simultaneously tried to keep the choking poison out of their lungs and check the hordes of Germans following behind the wall of gas. It was a hopeless situation. The fumes penetrated the wet handkerchiefs and again men and officers dropped to the ground, clutching their throats, writhing and vomiting in a slow and frightful agony of death. What happened next is unclear. We do know that a handful of men from each of the two companies survived the gas and shelling and stumbled back in disarray to a small wood by the Stroombeek. Here they dug in, as much as their physical condition would permit, and apparently decided to fight it out to the finish.[10]

At the middle levels of command various steps were taken to reinforce the threatened front. The first message reaching Turner's Headquarters at 4.30 AM erroneously reported that the left of the 2nd Brigade had been driven in. Turner, having no reserves, immediately released the 10th Battalion and then the 16th from south of Kitchener's Wood. The former, directed to move to Locality C,[11] arrived at 5.40 AM and extended in a shallow trench.

On learning of the direction of the attack, General Currie placed at the disposal of Lt.-Col. L.J. Lipsett of the 8th Battalion a reserve company from each of the 5th and 7th Battalions. At the same time Lipsett sent half of his own reserve company to the left to assist the 15th Battalion. He directed the other half to seal his open left flank. The latter two platoons drew machine-gun fire as they crossed a high bank to occupy a trench. Their leader was shot and a number of the men were hit. Sgt.-Maj. F.W. Hall brought two of the wounded back into the trench but groans of suffering indicated there was another helpless victim on the ridge. Corporal Payne and Private Rogerson volunteered to accompany Hall and the three men went over the parados. Payne and Rogerson were wounded almost instantly and with Hall's assistance crawled and scrambled back to the shelter of the trench. Hall rested a few minutes before attempting the rescue again. While he crawled slowly along the ground bullets ricocheted off the top of the parados in his rear and cut the ground around and in front of him. He moved up the slope of the bank where, guided by the weakening groans of suffering, he located the wounded man. He lay flat and squirmed beneath his helpless comrade, getting him on his back. As he glanced up to survey the ground over which he had to return to shelter, he was shot in the head and instantly killed. For his act of heroism Hall was awarded the Victoria Cross posthumously.[12]

While this was going on the Germans attacked the north-western face of the salient. Their initial effort was not preceded by any effective discharge of gas. Canadians between Keerselaere and Kitchener's Wood observed that the release of gas from the enemy's line was abruptly stopped owing, it seemed, to a slight shift in the direction of the wind. Little if any of the fumes reached the defenders. Once within range the Germans made excellent targets as they came on in close formation over practically level ground. A furious burst of rifle and machine-gun fire cut down wave after wave, leaving the dead and wounded lying in long rows. Reeling, the German infantry drew back to allow the artillery to subdue the defenders. Aided by observers who had a clear view from the Poelcappelle houses and undisturbed by British counter-batteries, German guns laid down a dense and deadly bombardment along the front between the apex and St. Julien. Whole stretches of trench were obliterated and casualties mounted rapidly.

By breaking through the 15th Battalion's line to a depth of some 700 yards the Germans were in a position to take in reverse the Canadians holding the north-western face of the salient. They chose not to do so for the time being. Instead they mounted further attacks southward, overran the little band in the woods by the Stroombeek and reached the outskirts of Locality C. Here they were twice repulsed by the garrison.

The Germans then accentuated their efforts to reduce the apex. While their infantry prepared to assault from all sides, their guns systematically shelled up and down the length of the trenches north-westward from St. Julien. The position of the defenders at the northern end of the salient became untenable. This was especially true of the 13th Battalion, which was without machine-guns, all put out of action by the shelling, and which was under heavy attack from the front and threatened from the rear. At 8.30 AM the order was passed down for the 13th to withdraw to a reserve line westwards of Locality C. The movement should have begun with the units at the tip of the apex but presumably the pressure of events dictated otherwise.

Three of the four companies of the 13th fell back in good order despite German artillery fire, described by one eyewitness as 'absolutely hellish in its accuracy.' The far right company under the redoubtable McCuaig was not nearly as fortunate. Now badly exposed and reduced to three officers and 40 men it stood no chance of getting out unscathed.

The moment McCuaig gave the signal the men dashed back toward the nearest cover, about 50 yards away. Only a few managed to scramble to safety. The Germans who had been expecting such a move, swept the open ground with intense rifle and machine-gun fire, cutting down most of the Highlanders before they had covered half the distance. It was then that Lieutenant Pitblado showed exceptional courage in carrying back Captain Whitehead, second-in-command, who had been mortally wounded and was delirious. Whitehead lapsed into unconsciousness and Pitblado was compelled to abandon him after being hit in the knee. As he struggled on he came face-to-face with McCuaig and the two men saw to the retirement of the remnant of the company. McCuaig's report, written after the war, described what followed:

We were going back together when I was wounded in the knee but was able to proceed. I was shortly after shot through both legs and rendered helpless. Pitblado in spite of my protests refused to leave me and bandaged up the wounds in my leg under a very heavy fire. He was then wounded a second time in the leg, which finished his chances of getting away. I was subsequently wounded four more times while lying on the ground. We both remained there until picked up by the Germans an hour or two later. Their firing line passed us about ten minutes after we were wounded. [13]

For McCuaig and Pitblado the war was over. The courage and devotion shown by these two men throughout the engagement were later acknowledged when they received respectively the Distinguished Service Order and the Military Cross.

At the end of the apex the company of Buffs, without a written order to retire, fought on alongside the left company (No. 4) of the 15th Battalion. Cut off, bombarded continuously and pressed on all sides by the enemy's infantry, the Buffs and Highlanders held out until 9.10 AM when, with ammunition exhausted and most of the survivors wounded, they surrendered.[14]

Around 8.30 AM, as part of their general attack across the whole front, the Germans again tried to advance up the Steenbeek to St. Julien. The results were the same as the last time. The St. Julien garrison had no difficulty in repelling the onslaught despite the jamming of the Ross rifles from the rapid fire. Farther west the enemy's bid to work in between the two companies of the 3rd Battalion and St. Julien was frustrated by rifle and machine-gun fire. Facing Kitchener's Wood the 2nd Battalion, which had gone into the line to relieve the 10th and 16th Battalions, was not seriously troubled by the enemy.

By mid-morning the Germans had accomplished the first phase of their plan, that is, the capture of the apex. An open stretch of nearly 1500 yards now existed from the left of the 8th Battalion south-westward to Locality C. Apart from cross-fire this gap was undefended, for the nearest Canadian infantry was a company (5th Battalion) at Boetleer's Farm, the sole remaining reserve of the 2nd Brigade.

With the gassed men and wounded streaming back into the centre of the salient the confusion at all levels of command was, if anything, greater that that of the evening of the 22nd. It was caused partly by lack of reports from the front line units of the 2nd and 3rd Brigades and partly by misunderstandings growing out of the failure of the com-

mand posts of both these formations to confirm their telephone conversations with signal messages. The consequence
of the early and frequently contradictory messages, examples
of which will be shown immediately below, was that Divisional Headquarters remained unsure of the location and
extent of the German attacks until 7.20 AM.

At 4.55 AM Turner advised Alderson that the left of the
2nd Brigade had collapsed[15] when in fact it was the right of
his own brigade that had given way—indeed 3rd Brigade
Headquarters did not discover the truth until 7 AM. A message from 2nd Brigade command post, delivered at 6.30 AM,
indicated that the 3rd Brigade line was crumbling and that
the situation was critical.[16] Twenty minutes later Turner sent
word that all was well: '2nd Bde. informs me 6.00 AM that
situation on right of this brigade is in hand and we are holding trenches.... Am in constant touch with 2nd Bde.... We
do not feel uneasy.'[17] Finally at 7.20 AM Turner informed
Alderson that his right was retiring,[18] a message he subsequently confirmed while requesting help.

Therefore at 7.40 AM Alderson ordered two battalions of
the 150th Brigade (50th Division), which had already come
under his command, from the Brielen area to man the GHQ
Line across the Ypres-Poelcappelle road, in support of the
2nd and 3rd Brigades.[19] An hour later, as the enemy continued pressing its attack on St. Julien, he directed the other
two battalions of the 150th to move forward to the GHQ
Line.[20] Alderson hoped to relieve the 3rd Brigade in the evening with these fresh troops and at 10.35 AM he urged Turner
not to call on the 150th unless absolutely necessary.[21]

The V Corps did not hear of the German break-in until
7.40 AM and even then had to wait nearly four hours before
receiving further news. At 11.33 AM a message from the
27th Division reported the new Canadian position after the
loss of the apex. Alarmed by the latest developments Plumer
ordered the Canadian Division to take instant action to recon-
stitute the line. Several hours earlier he had made available to

Alderson the 151st Brigade, then guarding the left flank west of the canal, and for the moment had no other troops under his hand. He could only promise that on arrival in the Ypres area the 4th Division's 10th Brigade would be at the disposal of the Canadians.

It is apparent from reading the various reports and diaries that the command structure in the threatened area was now breaking down. As misunderstandings, confusion, delays and often faulty reports spread a dense fog of war across the battle area it became impossible to co-ordinate the movements of the front-line units. Thus the burden of conducting the fighting fell mainly on the battalion commanders. These met periodically in groups of two or three to discuss common problems and share their resources. None had any idea of the general situation. The result was that their action reflected concern over local rather than overall conditions.

Shortly after 9 AM there was a lull in the fighting that lasted two hours. The Germans had sustained heavy casualties and needed time to sort out their units after their convergent attack. Around 11 AM they renewed their assault, heralding their advance by a massive bombardment of the entire Canadian line. Deployed in open formation they fell upon the battle-weary units of the 3rd Brigade in two successive attacks, the first from the north and the other from the north-west up the valley of the Steenbeek toward St. Julien.

After the loss of the apex the Canadian line from Locality C to the northern end of St. Julien was shaped like a rough semi-circle. It was manned by the 10th Battalion, resting near Locality C, followed by the remnants of the 15th, the 13th, No. 3 Company of the 14th and the 7th (less one company). Given no reinforcements, as none were available, these units were left to defend a position that was in perfect view of the enemy and enfiladed by machine-gun fire from both flanks.

Near Keerselaere the right two platoons of the 7th Battalion, decimated by six hours of uninterrupted shelling, were overrun.[22] That a far greater disaster did not occur was due to the valour of Lieutenant Edward D. Bellew, machine-gun officer of the 7th Battalion. Bellew had two of his guns in action on the high ground overlooking Keerselaere, slightly to the left of the right company. Sergeant H.N. Peerless handled one gun and, as his other men had been hit, he operated the other. When the front of the right company was penetrated, the two soldiers remained where they were and emptied belt upon belt of ammunition into the advancing enemy. Disgusted that their progress was being held up by the fire of two machine-guns, the Germans tried to work behind them. Peerless was killed. Bellew was struck down by a bullet, nevertheless he got up and kept on firing until the last belt was finished. Then smashing his gun he met the enemy with bayonet and rifle butt. He was overpowered and taken prisoner.[23] When released in December 1918 he learned that he had been awarded the Victoria Cross. Bellew was the first officer of the Canadian Expeditionary Force to have received that honour.

Being out of touch with 3rd Brigade Headquarters, the commanders of the 7th (Major V.W. Odlum), 14th (Lt.-Col. W.W. Burland)[24] and 15th (Lt.-Col. J.A. Currie) met at the crossroads between Locality C and St. Julien and decided to withdraw from their exposed position to a new line 300 yards south of Gravenstafel Ridge. The right half of the line, that is, the 13th and survivors of the 15th Battalions, taking advantage of the dead ground[25] behind the crest, carried out the movement without serious losses. On the other side of the line the 7th was compelled to fight every inch of the way as it fell back in small parties. But the Germans pressed on relentlessly and after noon caught up with the two left companies 500 yards north-east of St. Julien. Only a handful of Canadians escaped. The bulk of the men dug in knowing they had no chance against the charging grey waves. The survivors eventually surrendered when they ran out of ammunition or their rifle bolt had stuck.

From the trenches captured north of St. Julien, German fire, directed by balloon and aeroplane observers, swept the flat ground on the southern side of the Ridge. The untenability of the new Canadian position compelled Currie, Burland and Odlum to meet for another consultation. The three commanders had information, erroneous as it turned out, that the 8th Battalion was retiring from the original line. Aware of Turner's determination to maintain his position until help arrived, Odlum suggested a counterattack to recover the skyline and the toe of the Ridge. The proposal was judged hopeless and in the end it was decided to make a further withdrawal, this time 1000 yards in rear to an unmarked line north of the Wieltje-Gravenstafel road. It was none too soon, for the Canadians were being heavily pressed by the Germans.

The fighting retirement from the crest of the Ridge was carried out in successive stages, each party on falling back covered the withdrawal of the next. Far from wilting under the strain, the Canadians kept up a disciplined fire that caused the troops of the 51st Reserve Division to break off their attack to await further reinforcements.

As arranged the Germans held back their assault on St. Julien until their northern one was under way. Shortly after midday, when the Canadian withdrawal had exposed the right of the St. Julien garrison, they struck from three directions and blasted their way through the narrow village streets. On the left a segment of No. 4 Company of the 14th managed to extricate itself by using as cover some of the houses. But No. 2 Company of the 14th and No. 2 Company of the 15th with orders to hold St. Julien to the last man, fought on until all were killed, wounded or taken prisoner.[26]

It cannot be said that the attack on St. Julien came as a surprise. Before noon observers reported that masses of German infantry, followed by artillery, were moving south from Poelcappelle toward St. Julien. South of Kitchener's Wood the companies of the 3rd and 2nd Battalions could see line upon line of German infantry emerging from the dead ground for the assault against St. Julien.[27] News of this concentration reached Divisional Headquarters and caused a change in plans.

As mentioned earlier Alderson had sent the 150th Brigade forward to the GHQ Line in response to the retirement of Turner's right. Alderson's initial impulse to employ the 150th to replace the 3rd Brigade at the end of the day's fighting gave way to his conviction that the lost ground must be regained. At 11.35 AM he assigned two of the battalions to Turner with instructions to counter-attack with energy.[28] However, once alerted to the impending enemy assault on St. Julien, he countermanded this directive and instead ordered Turner to utilize the two battalions 'to strengthen your line and hold on.'[29] This was intended to mean the line of the 3rd Brigade from Locality C to Hampshire Farm. If Turner had any doubts it must have been cleared up in a telephone conversation with Colonel C.F. Romer, Alderson's GSO 1, at 1.35 PM. Yet five minutes later he directed the eight battalions (two British and six Canadians) under his command to hold the GHQ Line from the St. Jean-Poelcappelle road southward.[30] Duguid writes that Turner understood his instructions to mean that he should hold St. Julien as long as possible and then occupy the GHQ Line.[31] But Duguid was trying to protect Turner who was still alive when the official history was published.[32] The evidence shows that it was more than a misunderstanding; that in fact Turner wilfully disobeyed orders. Commenting on Turner's action, Lt.-Col. Gordon-Hall subsequently recalled:

It should ... be noted ... that this early Turner began to sit on his reserves instead of using them to reinforce his forward position as directed by Div. HQ. This policy he pursued to the end and nothing Div. HQ or other commanders could order, or suggest, or implore made him alter his policy, with of course disastrous consequences to all concerned and to none more than to his own troops.

I don't think enough is made of the overcrowding in GHQ Line and to the resultant heavy casualties from hostile artillery fire. It had a magnetic attraction for Turner in spite of the fact that it faced the wrong way and could be enfiladed.[33]

Turner's decision to fall back to the GHQ Line created a gap in the Second Army's flank through which a resolute German advance could have cut off the 2nd Canadian Brigade and the adjoining 28th Division. The 3rd Brigade was under heavy enemy pressure and one can understand Turner's concern for his men but he selected an alternate course that was infinitely worse. And he did so without notifying Currie, the person who was most adversely affected by his action. Turner's conduct was inexcusable on both counts and he was very fortunate to have escaped dismissal.

Needless to say Alderson was horrified by Turner's lapse of judgment, which threatened to produce a disaster of major proportions. After this day he would never again trust Turner, concluding that he was unfit for command in the field.[34] In view of his attitude why did he not send Turner home? Was it, given his compassionate nature, out of desire to avoid humiliating a national hero? Or was it because he was uncertain of how Ottawa would react? The last thing he wanted was to become embroiled in a controversial issue that might dampen the strong pro-British feeling in Canada. Whatever his motive he must be faulted for having tolerated insubordination, occurring as it did during a moment of battlefield crisis. 'Had we been a British Division and under the War Office,' wrote J. Sutherland-Brown, then Director of Military Operations and Intelligence, 'I am quite certain that either General Alderson or General Turner, or both of them, would have lost their commands.'[35]

Much of the correspondence exchanged between Divisional and Third Brigade Headquarters on 24 April cannot be found. In 1925 Sutherland-Brown gave his version of what occurred.

> If my memory serves me correctly ... General Turner came to Div. HQ shortly after we reached Nieppe [28 June, 1915] and evidently made some accusations against General Alderson and his staff concerning their treatment of the Third Brigade during the battle of Ypres.... The result of this..., I imagine, from the way things turned out afterwards, that they both buried the hatchet. It now became about the limit of the time for my curiosity to be satisfied and I asked Henry Lamb [General Staff, 1st Can. Div.] to let me see the report of the battle and the correspondence with the Third Brigade. The report of the battle was available but I was informed by Colonel Lamb that the correspondence had been destroyed.[36]

This is a possible, even likely, explanation but it does not square with the statements given by Alderson and Lamb to the Canadian Official Historian. While neither man could account for the missing correspondence both denied that it had been deliberately destroyed.

Now to continue with the story of the battle. On the Third Brigade's left, the 2nd and 3rd Battalions had successfully held up, and in the process taken a heavy toll on the enemy west of St. Julien. The 2nd Battalion from eastern Ontario was commanded by Lt.-Col. D. Watson. The 3rd Battalion was raised chiefly from three well-known Toronto militia regiments, the Governor-General's Body Guards, the 10th Royal Grenadiers and the Queen's Own Rifles. The battalion was under Lt.-Col. R. Rennie with its two front-line companies directed by Major A.J.E. Kirkpatrick. Early in the afternoon Turner's directive to fall back was passed verbally from platoon to platoon, causing confusion and dismay among the men. With things going astonishingly well on their own restricted front they could not understand the need

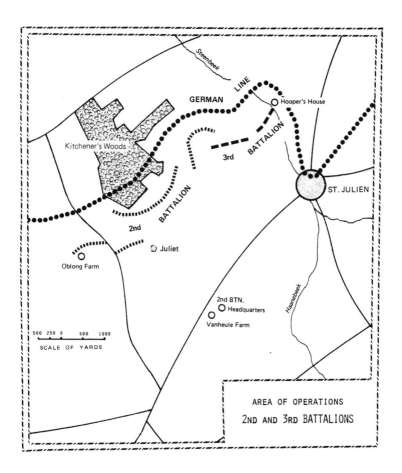

Steenbeek

GERMAN LINE

Hooper's House

Kitchener's Woods

3rd BATTALION

2nd BATTALION

ST. JULIEN

Juliet

Oblong Farm

Haanebeek

2nd BTN.
Headquarters
Vanheule Farm

500 250 0   500   1000
SCALE OF YARDS

AREA OF OPERATIONS
2ND AND 3RD BATTALIONS

to retire.

It was one thing to direct the two battalions to withdraw, quite another to extricate them directly from the face of the enemy. On some parts of the front the fighting was practically hand-to-hand and the ground immediately behind was open and swept by rifle and machine-gun fire. It seemed better to stand fast and kill Germans than to be shot in the back while running away. There were other instances in which isolated groups, their officers put out of action, suspected a ruse and refused to budge; or they were unsure of what they were supposed to do and by the time they reacted sometimes it was too late. George Patrick belonged to a unit that found itself isolated and without even an NCO. His recollections are worth noting.

Our company had left, and the little group that I was in didn't get word to go. I said, 'Well, let's get out of here.' My chum said, 'Nothing doing. We dug this hole and we are going to stay here.' Well another group came in from the other Brigades, and this officer who had brought them in asked me if I knew the orders. I said, 'No, I haven't any idea. But,' I said, 'the Adjutant and the Commanding Officer are back in that farm.' And he said, 'Will you go over and find out for me?' And finally I said, 'All right, I'll go.' ... I said, 'Excuse me, Mr. Turner, are we running away from this gang?' He said, 'Oh no, we are simply retiring to a prepared position.' I said, 'That's all right, that's fine.' So I went back and I said to my chum, 'Let's get out of here.'[37]

The CO of the 2nd Battalion, D. Watson, having seen to the removal of the wounded, left his headquarters to personally superintend the retirement of his companies. On arrival at the front he proceeded to pull his companies back, one by one—first the company on the left, then the centre company and lastly the company on the right. Watson remained with his second-in-command, Colonel Rogers, until the last company was on its way. Then the two officers shook hands and took separate routes, thinking that it would increase the chances of one of them getting through the enemy's pitiless fire. Running as fast as he could for about 300 yards, Watson paused for a moment under the cover of a tree. Glancing back he noticed that one of his officers, Lieutenant A.H. Hugill, was lying on the ground some 60 yards to the left. Assuming he was wounded Watson hurried over and asked what was wrong. Hugill replied that he was exhausted and needed a few moments to recover his breath before he could make another dash.

Hugill was barely back on his feet when Private Wilson of the 2nd Battalion, passing nearby, was shot through the leg. Watson asked Hugill if he was up to helping carry the wounded man over the remaining 700 or 800 yards of fire-swept ground. Hugill said he was, whereupon Watson knelt down and placed Wilson on his back. As Watson staggered along with his load the air was alive with bullets and flying shrapnel. After carrying the wounded private for what seemed an eternity but in reality was only several hundred yards Watson reached his battalion headquarters. By now the place was deserted. After resting for a few minutes they started off once more and the two officers between them managed to get Wilson back to safety. It was one of many such acts of heroism that went practically unnoticed that day.

By crawling along the ground and then taking advantage of such cover as was provided by buildings and hedges, a sizeable portion of the three companies of the 2nd Battalion threaded their way to the GHQ Line as directed. However, at both ends of the 2nd Battalion's front the garrisons of Oblong Farm and Hooper's House were too closely engaged to comply with the order. They remained in their position, firing steadily until they succumbed to superior numbers.[38]

Subjected to an intense fire from front and flanks the two companies of the 3rd Battalion under Major Kirkpatrick were similarly unable to break off and retire. They fought on knowing that only a counter-attack could save them. With the assistance of two machine-guns mounted in farm buildings east of Kitchener's Wood they hurled back one enemy assault after the other. At the height of the fighting something incredible happened to John Hewitt, a member of one of the machine-gun crews. A bullet went through his cranium and came out between his eyes. A witness describes what followed:

> I thought he was gone but he began to stir after a while and stood up on his rubbery legs. And I said, 'How do you feel, John?' 'Oh,' he said, 'I feel as if I had been on a drunk for a week.... That's all.' And he was able to march back with us.'[39]

By 3.30 PM only one machine-gun was in operation, ammunition was running low and the Germans were closing from both sides on the isolated trench. Of the 425 men who had moved into the line less than 100 could walk; the right company could muster only 43 soldiers, nearly every one of these was wounded and two were totally blind. The survivors had been fighting ceaselessly for 36 hours; they had gotten no sleep and they were drugged with fatigue. When the Germans sprang out of their trenches for one final rush the men of the 3rd Battalion knew that their day was done. Major Kirkpatrick wrote: 'For one moment, like gladiators we stood at gaze, then surrounded and outnumbered, our ammunition all but gone, we bowed to the inevitable and to save useless waste of life, gave in.'[40]

The movement of the 3rd Brigade to the GHQ Line coincided with the advance of British units south of Fortuin. At 9 AM that morning Plumer had given General Snow (CO, 27th Division) command of all the troops in corps reserve with power to use his discretion in employing them to meet unexpected local developments. Notification of his appointment does not seem to have reached subordinate commands.

Snow had information that the Germans had broken through at Berlin Wood—between the 2nd Canadian Brigade and the 85th British Brigade—and were in possession of Fortuin, a scattered group of farms and cottages about half a mile south-east of St. Julien. Unknown to him the line was still intact and Fortuin was being held by 200 Canadians, mostly remnants of the 7th and 10th Battalions. Operating in ignorance Snow directed the 1st Royal Irish Regiment from his own divisional reserve to march to Fortuin and drive back the Germans. Since additional troops could not be obtained from either the 27th Division or the V Corps, Snow commandeered two battalions (1st Suffolk and 12th London) from the 28th Division's reserve and sent them to join the Royal Irish. Simultaneously he directed General Turner, the senior officer on the spot, to take command of the three units and to use every man at his disposal to stop the enemy's advance from Fortuin.[41]

Turner was not aware that Snow's powers of command had been extended but it is unlikely that even if informed he would have reacted any differently. Snow, like Alderson, was calling for measures contrary to his designs. In the early afternoon Alderson repeatedly urged that the 3rd Brigade hold its ground as help was on the way and by 3 PM he had sent up from his reserve near Brielen Bridge the 4th Battalion (1st Canadian Brigade) and the 2nd KOYLI and Queen Victoria's Rifles (13th Brigade) to Wieltje and St. Jean to support Turner. The Commander of the 3rd Brigade paid no more attention to Snow's orders than he had to Alderson's. At 5.30 PM he walked over to Fortuin and directed the Royal Irish to withdraw to the GHQ Line at dusk. He saw no sign of the two battalions belonging to the 28th Division.[42]

It is difficult to find an explanation for Turner's conduct. Had he panicked and suffered a momentary lapse of judgment or was he simply unsuited for high command? By concentrating his forces in the GHQ Line he violated all sound

135

military principles. Although a solidly prepared line of defence, most of it faced east, even south of east. More serious, the abandonment of his position gravely endangered the left rear of the 2nd Brigade. One might understand Turner's reasoning if no alternative had existed. But there were three battalions in the vicinity with others on the way. He could have reinforced the threatened sectors of his front and while he may not have saved St. Julien he could have averted the slaughter of the 2nd and 3rd Battalions and maintained contact with the left of the 2nd Brigade.

Between noon and 2 o'clock the two battalions of the 150th Brigade, the 4th East Yorkshire and the 4th Green Howards, arrived at Potijze. Commanded by Lt.-Col. M.H.L. Bell they were destined to play a pivotal role in the action of the day. Alderson had sent them to help the 3rd Brigade cover the St. Julien area but along the way Turner had diverted them to the GHQ Line. Around 3 PM Bell received from a staff officer of the 27th Division orders similar to those given to the Royal Irish—to counter-attack and stop the enemy advancing from St. Julien. There were now five battalions directed on Fortuin. Thus while the various units of the 3rd Brigade were falling back toward the GHQ Line, five British formations fortuitously appeared in the gap and almost certainly avoided a major disaster.

Currie showed better leadership qualities than Turner in coping with the pressures on his front. All day the 2nd Brigade was in constant danger of being outflanked. After the first onslaught the 5th and 8th Battalions continued to hold firm in the original line, but an ominous opening existed on the left flank and the Germans were threatening to penetrate through it. To make matters worse Currie's command post was destroyed by artillery fire and he was forced to move his headquarters to the 2nd Artillery Brigade about 700 yards distant.

Currie had already sent all of his reserves and such troops as he could commandeer into the fighting line. He tried without success to get reinforcements from the 85th British Brigade on his right. Turning to Divisional Headquarters he was told that two battalions from the York and Durhams (otherwise known as the 150th Brigade) were advancing into his area to help if necessary. Currie then forwarded a situation report to Alderson and proposed a counter-attack to blunt the enemy's drive.

An hour and a half later (9.30 AM), when there was still no sign of the promised reinforcements, Currie sent his orderly officer, Lieutenant Murray Greene, back to Wieltje to meet them and make sure that one battalion at least was detailed to close the gap east of Locality C. Time was increasingly crucial and during the next hour the situation on the left became worse. At 10.50 AM Lipsett reported that the Germans had begun to move around the end of his battalion (8th) and were threatening to surround it. Thereupon Currie telephoned 3rd Brigade Headquarters, urging immediate relief or 'the whole front is lost.' Turner returned the call several minutes later and the two generals reached an understanding. When the York and Durhams arrived Turner was to counter-attack with one of the battalions toward Locality C, while Currie would use the other unit to reinforce his front. This conversation, together with Lipsett's assurance that he would hold the trenches to the last man, eased Currie's anxieties for the moment. Then at 11.40 AM came devastating news. Garnet Hughes (Turner's brigade-major) reported, on the strength of 'information from an unknown source,' that the two battalions of the York and Durhams had been ordered back to their brigade. In fact these units had not withdrawn and it is impossible to say how 3rd Brigade Headquarters came to believe that they were. The upshot was that Turner could not now provide assistance on Currie's left.

In view of the latest development Currie came to the reluctant conclusion that he must effect a partial retirement with the 8th Battalion to fall back to Locality C and Boetleer Farm and the 5th to conform and maintain touch with the left of the 85th Brigade in the original trench line at Berlin Wood. Lipsett felt he could hold on a while longer and he delayed implementing the order to withdraw, pending a special reconnaissance of his front. The first reports indicated that the German advance between the front line and Locality C had halted. At noon Lipsett called—miraculously the telephone line connecting 8th Battalion headquarters and Currie's command post was still intact—his chief and conveyed the news.[43]

The Germans had not launched any strong infantry attacks against the old trench line after the first attempts in the early morning, preferring to reduce the defence with a deluge of artillery and mortar bombs. But the Canadians showed no signs of wavering and the tenacity with which they clung to a tactically unsound position gave the Germans good reason to suspect a trap. The Duke of Albrecht's plan had not called for them to roll up the line until the centre of the attack had broken through St. Julien and Fortuin and secured the western edge of Zonnebeke Ridge. For that reason the battalions driving toward the gap (XXVII Reserve Corps), although facing a skeleton garrison, camped down in the fields north of Locality C and awaited events.

Currie knew that the respite was temporary and that once German pressure resumed the situation would be intolerable. By bearing down on Lipsett's flank and Locality C it was clear that the Germans aimed to envelop Gravenstafel Ridge from the northwest. This, Currie felt, could best be frustrated by a counter-attack mounted from the 3rd Brigade area. Such an attack was feasible now that the reinforcements were unquestionably at hand.

Shortly after twelve o'clock the 4th Green Howards (from the York and Durhams) arrived at Wieltje and Lieutenant Greene delivered Currie's message to the officer in charge, Colonel Bell. But Bell refused to comply with it. His orders stipulated that he was to support both the 2nd and 3rd Brigades as required and until he found out what proportions should go to each he would take no action. Green returned to 2nd Brigade Headquarters and told Currie what had occurred.

Currie found himself in a thoroughly exasperating predicament. There were plenty of troops in or marching toward the GHQ Line but these were unavailable while his own brigade was threatened with certain destruction. Urged by his staff, he decided to go back to the GHQ Line in an effort to obtain the reinforcements that were so desperately required. Currie took the extreme course of leaving his command post because he thought the York and Durham Battalions 'might move for me when unlikely to move for officers of lesser rank.'[44] However well intentioned, it was an ill-advised step. Even Hugh Urquhart[45] privately admitted that his hero had exercised poor judgment on this occasion, concluding that 'the General Currie of 1915 was not the Currie of 1918, or for that matter of 1916.'[46]

Before leaving, Currie contacted Lipsett, telling him what he proposed to do. Lipsett favoured the idea with the reservation that should the situation become critical he would act on Currie's previous retirement order. Currie agreed but told Lipsett that he was not to use it unless forced by circumstances. 'As he was the man on the spot,' Currie wrote, 'I left it to his judgment, and Lipsett and myself had a very clear understanding.'[47]

Currie's mission was unsuccessful. At the GHQ Line he found Colonel Bell who again refused to move his troops forward without orders from division. While there, Brig.-Gen. J.E. Bush, commander of the York and Durhams, arrived. Currie begged Bush to counter-attack from the area of the 3rd Brigade, disregarding the urgent need to reinforce his own front. Bush was ready to counter-attack but he wanted to wait for the second battalion (4th East Yorkshire), which he said was coming up by way of Potijze. He then left to meet the battalion and hurry it to the rendezvous.

Around 2 PM the 4th East Yorkshires arrived at the GHQ

139

Line and Currie urged them to advance toward St. Julien. They would not move, however, without instructions from their brigade commander. Just as Currie was on his way to try to find Bush he encountered Lieutenant H.F. McDonald, a member of Turner's staff, who passed the news that the 3rd Brigade had been ordered to retire to the GHQ Line. Currie could not understand why such action had been taken. As noted, Alderson, having received reports suggesting that the enemy was massing for an all-out assault on St. Julien, had cancelled the 3rd Brigade's counter-attack and instead ordered it to strengthen the line with the York and Durham Battalions and to hold on. Turner, presumably convinced that the Germans could not be stopped, ignored the directive and pulled his men a mile back, to the GHQ Line. The withdrawal left the 2nd Brigade's flank completely exposed and made Currie more anxious than ever to hurry forward the York and Durhams.

Currie caught up with Bush at a farm south-east of Wieltje. As much as he wanted to, Bush was powerless to help. He had received orders cancelling the counter-attack.

While at the farm Currie learned that there was a British Divisional Headquarters several hundred yards away. He assumed that from there he would be able to inform Alderson of the grave situation on his front.[48] Arriving around 3 PM Currie found out that it was the command post for General Snow who directed the 27th Division. Currie had never met Snow and he was unaware that he had been given control of all the troops in Corps reserve.

What followed was a stormy interview, the details of which were suppressed by the Canadian Official Historian as well as by Currie's biographer. Both had ample evidence—in particular the accounts of Currie and an eyewitness, Major E.F. Lynn of the Canadian Engineers. Duguid did write a summary of the meeting in an early draft of his history but omitted it in the final form, undoubtedly because of strong pressure from his British counterpart, Brig.-Gen. J.E.

Edmonds.[49] Urquhart was not under any restrictions, as far as is known, and his silence on the incident is a mystery.

As Currie entered the dugout of the Headquarters of the 27th Division his attention was drawn to a general sitting at a table immediately on the left of the door. It was General Snow. His elbows rested on some papers spread over the table and his hands were over his face. He was perhaps thinking about his interview several minutes ago with Captain P.F. Villiers, a Canadian officer on the staff of the 3rd Brigade. Having failed to elicit satisfactory replies to his questions, Snow had become abusive, shouting and cursing Villiers for his stupidity.[50] He was still upset and angry when he looked up and saw Currie standing in front of him. 'Well what now?' he bellowed in a loud raucous voice. Currie identified himself and added, 'I am being hard pressed at certain points.' With the aid of a map he proceeded to describe the tactical situation on his front.[51] Currie had no sooner mentioned that there was a gap between the 3rd Brigade and the left of his 8th Battalion when Snow began to shout, asking how dare he allow such a thing to occur. Currie would recall eleven years later: 'To hear him you would think that I personally and solely was responsible for that gap, though every man of the 2nd Brigade was fighting in the line at the moment.'[52]

Pausing briefly for the interruption Currie went on to say that it was essential to the safety of the whole line that the threatened areas be reinforced without delay. 'Your men are being directed to points in the line which are already well held and in safe keeping. I would suggest that they should be diverted to these points.' He simultaneously indicated them on the map. Currie further declared: 'Your men are fresh and their assistance at the points mentioned would be of great value.' On hearing Currie's remarks Snow flew into a rage: 'Have you come to teach me my profession and dictate to me how I shall handle my Division?' His following remarks, smothered as they were by his frenzied outburst, were so incoherent and unintelligible that it was impossible to form an estimate of what he intended to convey.[53] Currie suffered through Snow's temper tantrum in silence. When Snow's choleric explosion eventually subsided, more as a result of exhaustion than anything else, the dialogue continued:

> Currie: 'There was no intention on my part to attempt to teach you your job or to advise you how to handle your Division; but I have been in this sector for some time now and know it pretty well. My Brigade has been in the line for ten days. They were in it when the attack was launched, and have resisted every attack without relinquishing a foot of trench. They have counter-attacked and at many points have been fearfully cut up. They are tired and hungry and require support at many points before nightfall.'
>
> Snow: 'Do you expect me to wet-nurse your Brigade? You have got yourself and your men into a mess and you will have to get them out of it as best you can.'
>
> Currie: 'I am not in a mess nor are my men. My men and I have held out against fierce onslaughts and will continue to hold out so long as any of us are left. As I have already stated my men have not lost any ground despite the fact that they are played out, hungry and decimated. The support of some fresh troops is essential for the safety of the line.'

Snow interrupted before Currie finished: 'Enough of this, I have already heard enough of your harangue. Get out of here! Take care of your own line, you will get no help from me.'[54] Once more Snow started to shout and pour out invectives. Currie stiffened and his icy glare betrayed his contempt for Snow. As he walked away from the table Snow shouted 'Give them hell. Give them hell.' Currie wrote in retrospect: 'When I considered the position of all the troops of the 2nd Brigade and my inability to move two battalions whom I thought had been sent to our assistance, I confess that at that moment I thought I had never heard a more stupid remark.'[55] On his way out Currie sent off a situation report to

1st Division Headquarters, stating the facts as he believed them to be.

Dejected and bone-tired Currie paused outside of Snow's dugout. The Canadian officer who had been present during the interview walked over to Currie, stated why he was there and proceeded to take him to a group of stragglers nearby. Currie called out the men of the 2nd Brigade, formed them up and personally led them forward. As he approached the battlefront he placed them under a senior NCO who was a member of the party and ordered him to join the 8th Battalion. On learning that his command post had again been forced to move because of enemy shelling, Currie returned to his rear headquarters at Wieltje where he found his entire staff. During his journey important developments had occurred on the field.

On the way to attack and hold Fortuin the two units of the 28th Division, the 1st Suffolk and the 12th London (Lt.-Col W.B. Wallace), were instead diverted north-east to cover the flank of the 2nd Brigade. They advanced as far as the Zonnebeke-Keerselaere road when they ran into heavy fire, not only from Locality C, now in enemy hands, and the ridge to the west, but also from British artillery, which was unaware of the movement. They eventually entrenched south of the Haanebeek, facing Locality C. In the course of the action the Suffolks, in the lead, suffered 280 casualties while the 12th London lost 59, including its CO Lt.-Col. A.D. Bayliffe.

While Wallace's battalions were marching toward Gravenstafel ridge, the 4th Green Howards and the 4th East Yorkshires, acting presumably on Snow's orders, were moving northwards from Potijze. After silencing a machine-gun nest at a crossroads near Fortuin they saw large parties of Germans advancing southwards from St. Julien. Bell changed the front of the Green Howards quarter left to meet the enemy rush. He had no idea of the extent of the German assault but at the northern end of the GHQ Line troops of the

3rd Brigade under Lt.-Col. F.S. Meighen had a better view of the movement. They responded by firing with rifles and machine-guns into the long lines of Germans moving southeastwards from Oblong Farm and Kitchener's Wood. The rattle of musketry drew the attention of Lt.-Col. J.J. Creelman, artillery commander of the 2nd Brigade. From his headquarters south of Fortuin, he could see wave after wave of Germans advancing across the open fields from Kitchener's Wood. He at once ordered sections of the 5th and 6th Canadian Batteries into action. The gunners, firing over open sights, decimated the ranks of the oncoming Germans. The effect of the combined Canadian fire compelled the German right to take cover behind farm buildings and hedges. The remaining German force, out of range or sight, pushed on across the Wieltje-St. Julien road and collided with the York and Durhams. These British battalions, together with the Royal Irish, which had moved up through Fortuin, drove the Germans back on the village before stopping at the muddy channel of the Haanebeek. Believing that the British were attacking in strength, the Germans withdrew from St. Julien to a ridge on the north.

The British advance had come an hour too late to save the remaining detachments of the 2nd and 3rd Battalions between Kitchener's Wood and St. Julien. Nevertheless the tenacious resistance of these Canadians, followed by the appearance of fresh British battalions, served to prevent the execution of an order from the XXVI Reserve Corps to retake St. Julien that night. This was most fortunate for the gap had been partly reopened at 7 PM. As already recorded Turner had ordered the Royal Irish to fall back at dusk. They passed the word to the York and Durhams and all three battalions withdrew to the GHQ Line.

Throughout the day reinforcements from various quarters, among them the 151st Brigade (Durham Light Infantry) and the 10th Brigade, were hurrying into the Canadian sector. At Chateau des Trois Tours Alderson had planned to relieve

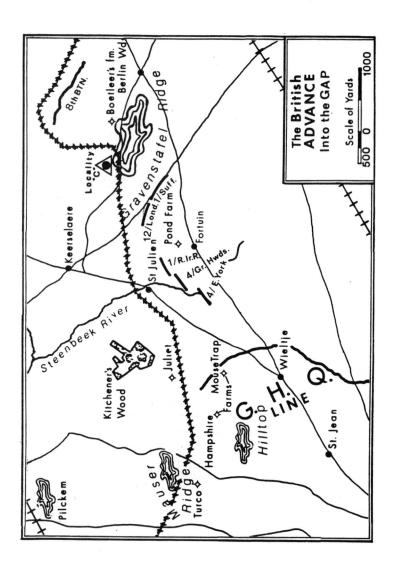

The British
ADVANCE
Into the GAP

Scale of Yards

500   0   1000

8th BTN.

Boetleer's fm.
Berlin Wd.

Locality "C"

Gravenstafel Ridge

Keerselaere

St Julien
12/Lond.1/Surr.
Pond Farm

Fortuin

1/R.Ir.R.

4/Gr. Hwds.

4/E.York.

Steenbeek River

Kitchener's
Wood

Juliet

Mouse Trap
Farms

Hampshire

Hilltop

G. H. Q.
LINE

Wieltje

St. Jean

Mauser Ridge

Turco

Pilckem

Geddes' Detachment and Turner's men that evening with the 10th Brigade and the uncommitted York and Durham Battalions. Shortly after 4 PM he received word of the withdrawal of the entire 3rd Brigade and its attached battalions to the GHQ Line. The message undoubtedly upset him but it could not have come as a complete surprise. Earlier in telephone conversations both he and his staff had tried to persuade Turner to follow a bolder strategy and to use the troops being sent forward to strengthen his line between Oblong Farm and Locality C.

At 4.35 PM Alderson ordered Turner to check the German advance with the battalions in and around Wieltje. He went on to say: 'You must push troops up into your front line and prevent at all costs the Germans breaking through between you and the 2nd CIB.' He admitted that he had 'no exact knowledge of your situation' but hoped that 'you are still blocking St. Julien and in close touch with 2nd CIB.'[56]

By late afternoon there were a medley of troops belonging to no less than eight battalions, crowded into the GHQ Line. For the most part they were disorganized, weak, tired and unfit for employment in attack. The two York and Durham Battalions, on which Alderson had placed much reliance, were then hotly engaged south-west of St. Julien. Turner could have, if he had wanted to, dispersed some units along the gap but he would have been hard pressed to mount any kind of sustained attack. At any rate he attempted neither. Ultimately Alderson's plan was set aside on account of the British Command's reaction to the tactical developments already described. Before relating this episode it might be helpful to examine the latest events on the French front.

French gains on the 24th had been negligible but at least they had not lost more ground. On their left they had established firm touch with the Belgians whose timely advance frustrated a renewed German attempt to take Zuydschoote. General Codet's men penetrated Lizerne around 2 PM but shortly thereafter were driven out. General Roy's bid to recapture Het Sas was equally unsuccessful. On the other hand the Germans failed to enlarge their bridgehead on the western bank of the canal.[57]

On the left of the British, four battalions of Zouaves advanced from the canal at 1.30 PM with the object of pushing the line forward toward Pilckem. Although Canadian batteries nearby assisted, the total weight of shells was insufficient to break down the resistance of the well-entrenched enemy. Later in the day the Zouaves, whose patrols had found Turco Farm unoccupied, took over the entire sector between the canal and Pilckem road. Turco Farm was designated as the point of junction between the French and British armies.

British plans were shaped, not only by what the enemy might do, but by the action of the French. Foch and his generals had promised to counter-attack to regain the lost ground but as yet there was no sign of the French infantry reinforcements or of the heavy guns so necessary for any hope of success. The British V Corps, which was supposed to play a subordinate role, had shouldered the entire burden, suffering losses out of all proportion to its gains. Plumer realized that it was his duty to fight on as long as possible to allow the French time to recover their balance. If the French meant to do nothing, however, it might be best to evacuate what was left of the salient, which was completely dominated by the enemy's artillery. British efforts could then be directed to expelling the Germans from the west side of the canal where they had but a tenuous hold. But it was Sir John French who settled the future course of operations. At 4.15 PM he sent a staff officer to Second Army Headquarters with the following message: 'Every effort must be made at once to restore and hold the line about St. Julien, or situation of the 28th Division will be jeopardized.'[58]

Toward the end of the afternoon Foch came to see Sir John and told him that the 153rd Division was detraining at Cassel and that a second division would arrive in time to participate in the joint operation. 'We will take a vigorous offensive against the front Steenstraat, Pilckem, Langemarck and east of these places,' Foch assured French.[59] Foch's goals were unrealistic. In all he had four divisions, two of which were exhausted, and a few field guns. With these effectives he proposed to drive four German divisions, covered by massive artillery fire, not only out of an entrenched position but back three miles to the original line. Sir John was less optimistic although he underestimated the strength and condition of the German forces. He was uncertain whether he could stop their advance from the north and he remained apprehensive about General Putz's left. He placed General Allenby's Cavalry Corps at the disposal of Putz to guard the Franco-Belgian junction.

At 6.30 PM General Plumer, who had been informed of Sir John's decision, instructed Alderson to launch the strongest possible counter-attack to retake St. Julien and re-establish the line. For that purpose he allocated the 10th and 150th Brigades and six battalions[60] or such of them as could be assembled under a selected commander. Alderson was told that if he needed additional forces he could call on the 149th and 151st Brigades, which were due to arrive that evening in the vicinity of Potijze in corps reserve. The hour of the attack was left to Alderson to decide with the proviso that it should not be delayed any longer than he considered necessary for reconnaissance and preparation.[61]

On receipt of Sir John's directive, Alderson cancelled the arrangements he had made to relieve the 3rd Canadian Brigade and Geddes' Detachment with the 10th and 150th Brigades. He appointed Brig.-Gen. C.P.A. Hull of the 10th Brigade to command the counter-attack. Given the time required to marshall the widely scattered force and arrange for artillery support with the Canadian and 27th and 28th Divisions, it was calculated that the operation could not begin until the early hours of the 25th. Alderson set the hour at 3.30 AM to reduce the effectiveness of the enemy's artillery.

At 8 PM he issued formal orders for the operation.[62]

The evening of 24 April was dark with heavy rain falling, exacerbating the confusion produced by contradictory or misinformed reports. The Germans, having had enough of fighting for one day, were quiescent, except for occasional attempts in the darkness to envelop and roll up the left of the 2nd Brigade. Colonel Lipsett took advantage of the relative lull on his front to seek out help from all likely sources, British and Canadian. His insistent appeal to the commander of neighbouring British units, who was himself hard pressed, met with understanding and at 8 PM a party of 100 2nd Northumberland Fusiliers arrived. Two platoons entrenched on the left of the 8th where, with the aid of a machine-gun, they were instrumental in breaking up three enemy assaults. The remainder took up a position southwest of Boetleer Farm. Upon learning that the Suffolks were behind Locality C, Lipsett pried two companies from Colonel Wallace and deployed them on the crest immediately west of Boetleer's Farm. These were joined by other units—a company of 1st Monmouthshire, a company of 2nd Cheshire and two half companies of the 8th Middlesex—provided by the 28th Division in response to Lipsett's earnest request. After midnight the weary remnants of the 7th and 10th Battalions, each numbering about 150 men, under Major Odlum, were brought up from the GHQ Line and continued the front westwards to the Haanebeek. With these reinforcements Lipsett established a tenuous defence line along the 2nd Brigade's left flank.

While Lipsett was straining every nerve to secure and extend his left, the 3rd Brigade and the troops that reinforced it,[63] some 3500 in all, occupied the GHQ Line from the St. Jean-Poelcappelle road northwards to Hampshire Farm. At 8.45 PM Turner informed Alderson of his position and added: 'Some of our troops still are in St. Julien surrounded, this number originally 700 now possibly 200.'[64] Turner's information was incorrect. The Germans had evacuated St.

Julien at 6.30 PM and the only troops there were the dead on both sides.

Turner was silent on the issue of re-establishing contact with the left of the 2nd Brigade. Although his orders had specifically instructed him to do so, he decided that it was not his responsibility. That honour belonged to General Snow who commanded the reserves and had the authority to use them to stop the German advance southwards. Presumably he was taking appropriate counter-measures.

Turner's messages to 27th Division Headquarters in the evening[65] alerted Snow that a grave misunderstanding had occurred. He notified the V Corps, which in turn dispatched a wire to General Alderson shortly before midnight. Plumer did not conceal his displeasure at the order that sent the 3rd Brigade and its attached units back to the GHQ Line. This meant, he went on to say, giving up all the ground 'for which such a struggle has been made today' and leaving the 2nd Brigade's flank in the air. He ordered instant action to re-establish the line as far forward as possible in the direction of St. Julien and in touch with troops on both flanks. If necessary Alderson was to appoint an officer to take command.[66] Curiously enough Plumer made no reference to the forthcoming attack by Hull whose resources were likely to be affected by this latest development.

Alderson was at a loss to understand the apparent inconsistency between his own instructions to Turner and Plumer's revelations of a serious breach in the line west of St. Julien. He sent Lt.-Col. Gordon-Hall forward with plenary powers to take what action was necessary to straighten out the tactical situation. Meanwhile Turner, baffled by the attitude and directives of GOC 27th Division, set out for the Chateau des Trois Tours on a motorcycle pillion to ascertain exactly from whom he was supposed to take his orders. There is no known record of the interview between Turner and Alderson. Apparently there were sharp exchanges and the meeting ended on a discordant note. Each was left with the impression that the other did not comprehend what was happening.

By the time Turner emerged from Alderson's Headquarters the troop movements at the front had ceased for the night. The Germans were dug in north of St. Julien and faced a British line that was very ragged and in places unguarded. A gap of two and three-quarter miles divided the 3rd Brigade from where the 8th and 5th Battalions, their trenches and shelters crowded with gassed and wounded men, were still holding fast. In this opening there were only two detachments: one a mixed force of Suffolks, Northumberland Fusiliers, Cheshires, Monmouthshires and Odlum's Canadians, occupying about 800 yards near Boetleer Farm; the other, a battalion of 12th London and two companies of Suffolks, manning an isolated 1200-yards-long section of the Gravenstafel road. The survivors of the 3rd Brigade and the various units sent to reinforce it were in the GHQ Line north of Wieltje, whence Geddes' Detachment and the 13th Brigade prolonged the line toward the canal. Thus the day that began ominously, with the shadow of defeat, ended with the situation more or less in hand. The Canadians had lost the apex of the salient, Locality C and St. Julien but at the same time they had thwarted the enemy's intention to press forward to Zonnebeke ridge. Because of the turmoil and absence of information they tended to regard the state of affairs as more serious than was actually the case. They were unaware of the tremendous punishment they had inflicted upon the enemy. The Germans had no fewer than 39 battalions opposite the right of the Canadian front, from Gravenstafel to Kitchener's Wood. An advance during the night when the frontage between Locality C and Mouse Trap Farm contained only a few British battalions would have brought them the victory they were seeking. That they did not do so is striking testimony to the reception their attacking waves had met all along the line throughout the day. Having been held to a standstill, they had lost some of their ardour. For the Canadians the worst was over.

Throughout the night of 24-25 April Hull was unable to establish the precise disposition of the enemy and he could not ascertain whether St. Julien had fallen or was still partially held. Hull and his officers did not know the terrain and there had been no time during the remaining daylight (that is, after 8 PM when the operation order was issued) for reconnaissance. Hull's plan was based on what he could glean from the map, supplemented by the information of several of Alderson's aides who were familiar with the area. These Canadian officers told him, so far as they knew, that the enemy occupied Kitchener's Wood and the trench on the outskirts, Oblong and Juliet Farms, and was probably in possession of St. Julien.

In darkness and in an area devastated by fire and intersected by trenches, it was by no means certain whether all the fifteen battalions detailed for the attack could be found and assembled. Initially only one of the battalion commanders appeared at the rendezvous, prompting Hull to postpone the attack until 4.30 AM. Proceeding to Wieltje he set up temporary headquarters in the ruins of a cottage and subsequently moved to Mouse Trap Farm where he remained during the battle. Conferring with his own battalion commanders he found that there were only two openings in the wire of the GHQ Line through which his brigade and half of the 150th would have to defile. The difficulties caused by this, together with the congestion of traffic on the road, compelled Hull to delay the operation for yet another hour. Even then Hull found himself with only the five battalions of his own 10th Brigade. Of the remaining ten battalions some did not receive their orders while others, although notified, were delayed on the road or were absent from their places at 5.30 AM.

Hull placed his four regular battalions in the first line and his Territorial unit in support behind the left. The 10th Brigade was fresh and at war-strength but it was called upon, like the 13th Brigade two days before, to accomplish the impossible. Hull's men were being sent over unknown and unreconnoitred ground to eject an enemy amply provided with machine-guns, lodged in ready-made cover in ruined houses and thickets and backed by massive artillery fire from the high ground behind. To make matters worse they received inadequate artillery support. The batteries of the 27th and 28th Divisions, ignorant of the postponement of the time of attack, fired their preliminary bombardment two hours earlier. Because of a mistaken report by General Turner that perhaps as many as 200 Canadians were still in St. Julien, a warning had been issued not to shell the village.[1] Several of the British batteries assigned to assist did not receive the message. They laid their guns on St. Julien, thus announcing to the enemy that there were no British troops there. Around 4.30 AM the German 51st Reserve Division, after its patrols confirmed that the place was deserted, proceeded to set up machine-guns in the outlying houses.

A thick morning mist shielded the five British battalions as they marched out in fours from the GHQ Line. Before they could form up they encountered first sniping and then a rapidly increasing volume of rifle and machine-gun fire. The brigade fanned out into fighting formation somewhat earlier than intended and, in faultless order, advanced against Kitchener's Wood and St. Julien. The men in the leading waves ran into such a frightful tempest of fire that they fell like wheat before a scythe. An inexperienced officer peering through his field glasses and seeing no forward movement, inquired 'Why do they stop?' There was a terse reply: 'They are dead.'[2] The following lines were pinned to the ground and each time they rose to advance they met the same reception. With the object of lending additional weight to the attack on the right, Hull ordered two battalions of the 149th (Northumberland) Brigade into action. These units lost their direction and instead of reinforcing the front ahead veered to the right and stumbled into enemy machine-gun nests. By 7 AM the British attack had broken up and the survivors were surging back in search of cover. When the supports arrived a new line was formed, running from a point west of Mouse Trap Farm to south of Fortuin where it linked up with the entrenchments of the two York and Durham Battalions. The operation had virtually annihilated the 10th Brigade, which lost 73 officers and 2346 other ranks in less than two hours.[3] Although Hull's men had failed to reach their objectives they had at last closed the gap in the St. Julien quarter and, as will be shown below, seriously disrupted the Duke of Albrecht's plans.

The experience of the 23rd and 24th had convinced Albrecht that he must stop the unprofitable offensive across the Yser and instead shift the main effort to the sector of the XXVIth Reserve Corps where it seemed possible to cut off the British position in the salient. The idea now was to drive southward through St. Julien with subsidiary attacks by the XXVIIth Reserve Corps' right wing against the northeastern part of the salient. But the striking power of the 51st Reserve Division (XXVIth Reserve Corps), charged with delivering the main blow, was expended in repelling Hull's assault. The right of the XXVIIth Reserve Corps went ahead, as scheduled, with its converging attacks—one westwards against the face of the salient at Broodseinde, the other southwards against the Gravenstafel Ridge.[4]

The Germans heralded their first assault on the morning of the 25th with an eight-hour bombardment that swept and searched the trenches of the 84th and 85th British Brigades (28th Division). Apart from shrapnel and high explosive, the Germans used gas shells, which seriously affected many of the men. Then at 1 PM a regiment of the 53rd Reserve Division charged across the 70 yards of no man's land on a quarter-mile front north of Broodseinde and reached the trenches occupied by the 2nd East Surreys. There was hand-to-hand fighting and the Germans broke in at several places. The battalion

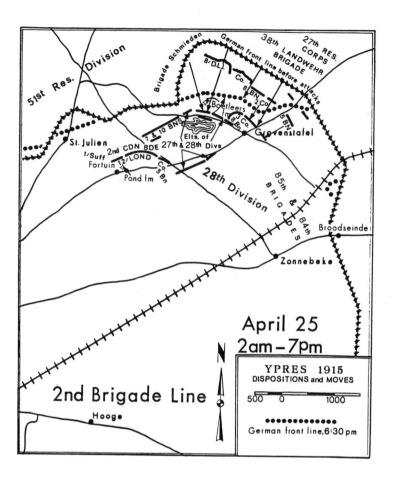

51st Res. Division

27th Res. CORPS

38th LANDWEHR BRIGADE

German front line before attacks

Brigade Schmieden

8/D.L.I.

Co.

8/ BN

2 Co.

3 Co.

5 BN

Boetleers

1 & 8 Bn

7 & 10 BNS

Elts. of 27th & 28th Divs

Gravenstafel

St. Julien

2nd CDN BDE

1/Suff

Fortuin 12/LOND

Pond fm

C 5 Bn

28th Division

85th & 84th BRIGADES

Broodseinde

Zonnebeke

April 25
2am–7pm

N

2nd Brigade Line

Hooge

YPRES 1915
DISPOSITIONS and MOVES

500   0   1000

●●●●●●●●●●●●●●
German front line, 6:30 pm

supports and an attached company of the 8th Middlesex counter-attacked at once, recovering most of the line and capturing 29 prisoners. The Germans remained in possession of 60 yards of breastwork despite two subsequent attempts to dislodge them.[5]

The Germans were equally active in the adjoining sector from early morning onwards. Artillery of all calibres pounded the 2nd Brigade's front line and ridge from Boetleer Farm to Gravenstafel, the shelling gradually increasing in volume and reaching a crescendo between 9 AM and noon. German machine-gunners, located in the houses of Locality C and along the road from St. Julien, swept the Stroombeek valley with enfilading fire.

During the night the 8th Durham Light Infantry (151st Brigade) under Lt.-Col. J. Turnbull arrived at Boetleer Farm. Sent by General Snow from the corps reserve at Potijze to assist the 85th Brigade (Brig.-Gen. A.J. Chapman), the unit had been ordered to act with the 1st Suffolk and 12th London to close any gap that might exist to the north. Although Turnbull considered himself responsible to General Chapman, and not to Colonel Lipsett, he agreed to replace the 8th Battalion, which was greatly reduced in numbers, weak from want of food and worn out by 48 hours of incessant fighting and bombardment. The coming of daylight prevented the systematic clearing of the dead and wounded from the trenches and the relief of the right company (No. 4) which remained in the line.[6] Two companies of Durhams (A and D) occupied the left of Lipsett's front while the other two were deployed in support along the hedges near Boetleer Farm. The three relieved companies of the 8th Battalion were then taken into reserve a short distance to the south-east, behind the crest of the ridge.[7]

Around 11 AM large bodies of German infantry were seen advancing from the direction of Poelcappelle and by 3 PM the assault was under way. The ordeal for the Durhams was particularly severe. Coming straight from home they had no time to become acclimatized to the mental and bodily torment of trench warfare before they were plunged into the horrors of the salient.

Turnbull, anticipating that pressure would be greatest on his extreme left, ordered one of his support companies forward. That company was unable to reach the front, caught as it was over the open valley by a blast of fire. Stunned and confused by the unexpected turn of events, the men retired again on Boetleer Farm, the German fire following them step-by-step. A Canadian who witnessed the scene recalled:

I have never seen such slaughter in my life. They were straight from England. They had never heard a shot fired in anger. They were lined up—I can see it still—in a long line—straight up and the Hun opened up on them with machine-guns. They were just raked down. It was pathetic.[8]

The Germans penetrated behind the three left companies in the British line but the fire of the Durhams, supplemented by the 8th Canadians, kept them at bay. Farther down the line the battalions of Brigade Schmieden pressed hard and gained a foothold at Boetleer Farm. To meet this threat Lipsett ordered his three reserve companies forward to the crest north and east of the farm.[9] There with the various British detachments—8th Durhams, Suffolks, Monmouths, Middlesex, Cheshires and Northumberland Fusiliers—they stopped the German infantrymen dead in their tracks. During the fighting many Canadians discarded their jammed Ross rifles and picked up the Lee Enfields of fallen British comrades.

To Alderson the latest German attempt to bite off the north-eastern apex came when his position had improved immeasurably. The 10th Brigade and attached battalions had filled the wide gap south of St. Julien. Although most of the Canadian units were terribly reduced and weary he still had three fresh battalions of the Northumberland Division; and there were three more, as well as a regular battalion, in Corps reserve. Furthermore he had been advised by V Corps Headquarters that both the 11th Infantry Brigade (4th British Division) and the Lahore Division were on their way to Vlamertinghe. By way of encouragement Alderson informed Currie at 11.50 AM that 'strong reinforcements' were coming up to his assistance. [10]

Alderson had recent and correct information that the 2nd Brigade's front, although under heavy pressure, was still intact. Air reconnaissance showed that the line further west was almost continuous. But in fact the trenches running from St. Julien eastwards to Locality C were occupied by the Germans, not by the 1st Canadian Brigade as was supposed. [11] Before this became known Alderson's hopeful thoughts were disrupted by several alarming messages. The first reported that the left front of the 28th Division was being attacked in force. The second stated that the enemy was advancing in long columns in the area north-west of the line Locality C-Boetleer Farm, which was tantamount to saying that Gravenstafel Ridge had been lost. Alderson at once communicated with both Hull and 2nd Brigade Headquarters at Wieltje to ensure that the news was transmitted to General Currie. [12]

Before the day's action began Currie was at 8th Battalion Headquarters sizing up the tactical situation. Having settled some pressing matters he left to establish his command post at 5th Battalion headquarters near Gravenstafel Cross Roads. The manner of his reception was not one that he wanted repeated. Standing beside the 5th Battalion CO, Lt.-Col. G.S. Tuxford, F.G. Bagshaw, then orderly sergeant, explained what happened:

> We saw a man on the height of land walking along the ridge from the 8th Battalion, and presently this fellow jumped down into a sap and came along the line into our battalion. And he said, 'Tuxford, who the hell was shooting at me?' And this was Currie. [13]

Throughout the day Currie, trying to cope with developments on his front, directed and encouraged his commanders. The situation was not reassuring. The 2nd Brigade's line was exposed and tactically unsound. Currie hoped that the promised counter-attack would clear the enemy off the toe of Gravenstafel Ridge and secure his left. But around 1 PM he learned that Hull's attack had been unsuccessful. To compound his anxiety no reinforcements had come up to fill the gap west of Boetleer Farm, though he was told to expect both the 1st Canadian Brigade and the rest of the 151st Brigade.[14]

The extreme left of the 2nd Brigade's front faced Locality C and was held by Odlum's 7th and 10th Battalions, now reduced to mere skeletons. The Germans were massed on the higher ground of Locality C and their artillery and machine-guns swept the Canadian trenches from front and flanks. There was much concern in Currie's headquarters lest a determined enemy assault overwhelm the thin Canadian line, which was unsupported by reserves and artillery.

For the moment at least Odlum's position was in no danger. His men had been subjected to heavy fire but not attacked. The only activity occurred early in the morning when two men were seen coming from a ruined house directly in front. Several shots rang out and they fell to the ground, apparently wounded. Someone in the line shouted that they were British and two Canadian soldiers ran forward to investigate. Fired on in turn these two men were hit but managed to hobble back to their line. On the left, where it was reported the Suffolks lay, a small group assembled and began exchanging shots with the Canadians. The distance between the two sides was only about 200 yards but the mist was so dense that Odlum was unable to determine whether those ahead were German or British troops. He ordered his men to cease firing. A young private, claiming to speak German, volunteered to go forward and find out who they were. He held up his hands and advanced, shouting in German. He had gone about 50 yards when he was struck down. There was no longer any doubt that those on the other side were Germans. By now their numbers had increased considerably and, although they tried to advance, they were stopped immediately and driven to the ground by rifle fire.[15] At 2 PM Odlum sent word to Currie that his men were almost done in but that they could hang on until nightfall providing the enemy did not mount a strong attack.[16]

In the centre of the line pressure intensified as the afternoon wore on. At 4 PM Currie was alerted that A and D companies of the Durhams had fallen back to the ridge. Currie reported the withdrawal to, among others, General Hull, from whom he requested troops for a counter-attack.[17] Half an hour later Currie received from Captain G.A. Stevens of the 8th Durhams a note that contradicted the earlier intelligence. In it Stevens wrote that, although all the men in the left front trench had been killed or wounded and one reserve company driven back, the line from Boetleer Farm to the road east of it was still intact. He added that the enemy did not appear to be pressing the attack except by artillery fire.[18] But all hopeful signs were dashed through receipt of two Canadian Division messages (relayed by 2nd Brigade Wieltje Headquarters) around 5 PM.

The first of these suggested that the Durhams had fled from the front and that No. 4 Company of the 8th Battalion had been surrounded and destroyed. This piece of intelligence was inaccurate. The three companies were still holding out in their allotted places, though they were surrounded on three sides and out of touch with the ridge. The other note announced that the 151st Brigade would not be available to reinforce Currie's battalions but would occupy a switch line from Gravenstafel to Fortuin and that one battalion for this task was already on the way.[19] Alderson's object in diverting the 151st Brigade was to permit Wallace's detachments to return to the 28th Division. Currie, however, interpreted the message to mean that his exposed position had been judged hopeless.

Taking everything into account—that is, the condition of his front, cancellation of reinforcements and implication that Gravenstafel Ridge was to be abandoned—Currie decided to retire southwards to the new line. Tuxford insisted that the troops could not withdraw until dusk and so did Lipsett who arrived at 5th Battalion headquarters just as the runners were setting out with the evacuation order for their units. But Currie was adamant, saying that the movement had to be carried out at once. 'God help us all,' Bagshaw wrote in his diary. 'It is madness to go before dark.'[20] The same order was conveyed to Lt.-Col. Turnbull of the 8th Durham but, uncertain as to which commander he was under, remained in position along the road east of Boetleer Farm; as did a company of 8th Middlesex and two and a half companies of the 1st Monmouthshire, sent up at this time by General Chapman.

Unknown to those on the ridge, the survivors of A and D companies of the Durhams and No. 4 Company of the 8th Battalion remained in their trenches, fighting gamely against overwhelming odds. Cut off from their battalions and under an artillery barrage that was increasing in fury, the three company commanders met shortly after 5 PM and agreed that they must retire to the ridge. A message was dispatched to ask if they could withdraw but no answer came. Nevertheless the operation proceeded, the first to go were small groups of wounded and gassed men. These disabled soldiers had to make their way rearward over a long stretch of open country upon which a torrent of fire was being directed. All but a few were mowed down before they reached the crest. To cover the withdrawal a platoon of the left company was sent to occupy a small house a short distance to the west. As the men crawled through a beetroot field a party of Germans, lying amid foliage on slightly higher ground, sprang up and took them prisoner.

The Germans, aware that something was in progress,

turned a concentrated fire on the front line, shelling it heavily and raking it with machine-guns. While a handful of Durhams remained behind to draw the enemy's attention the rest of the left company moved eastwards along the trench and made its way back successfully. A much harsher fate awaited the right company. Assaulted from all sides it was annihilated practically to a man.

No. 4 Company of the 8th Battalion was still in the line when it was rushed and surrounded. All the machine-guns had been silenced except one that was being effectively operated by Sergeant W.A. Alldritt.[21] He continued to fire into the advancing crowds of Germans until he was overpowered. Initially it was thought that only a few men, led by Sergeant Knobel, had managed to escape. As it turned out others, scattered here and there, survived the German onslaught. One such survivor, A.H. Fisher, discussed the aftermath in these terms.

We were at the apex so we got cut off. They cut through us at both sides.... I crawled through this hawthorn hedge and then when I came out I saw some other fellows, you see, so I just hooked up with them. And there was an officer there. I don't know who he was, but whoever he was he should have got a decoration for what he did. There had been a parapet thrown up there and he collected everyone of us at the back of it. We still had our rifles, you see. And he said, 'Now stay where you are and don't fire.' And we stayed there, and by then there must have been 200 of us collected from the [8th Battalion], 5th Battalion and a few other battalions. And then after that Fritzie got more confident of his position and he just came forward and then we had the order to let go. And we let go, and they must have thought the whole Canadian Army was at the back of it. It was an absolute surprise to them. But we held them up until dark and they couldn't go forward any more.[22]

The first groups to leave their trenches in the 2nd Brigades' front did so practically en masse and not successively from the left as had been arranged earlier. Unhampered, the Germans closed in on the 5th Battalion's two front-line companies and prevented them from falling back beyond the Gravenstafel Ridge where their reserve companies and those of the 8th had already retired. Tuxford, who was in the rear, collected 40 or 50 men from various units and started up the hill in order to help his beleaguered companies. Suddenly from a cottage 400 yards away a German machine-gun opened up and everyone scrambled for cover. Changing the belt took about a minute so that the men lay down while the machine-gun was firing, got up and ran 50 or 60 yards as soon as it ceased. Half way up the hill there was a loud explosion and the firing stopped. Tuxford turned toward the house where the machine-gun was placed in time to see it disintegrate into a cloud of flying debris. A British battery unit, firing behind Tuxford's right, had scored a direct hit.

Tuxford placed his men in the trenches on top of the hill and then sent word for the two companies to break off action. Soon the 5th Battalion appeared with A company of the right and B company on the left. The movement proceeded in good order despite the fact that the Germans were in hot pursuit, yelling and beating drums. Tuxford posted Sergeant Bowie and six men to guard his left at a distance of 80 yards from the main body. Bowie had barely established himself when he saw a party, which he estimated to number 150, appear over a rise ahead. Since he could not determine whether they were friend or foe he immediately issued a challenge. Back came a reply 'Do not shoot, ve was French.' Bowie shouted, 'Fire' and the Germans who were caught in the open, were cut to pieces. Bowie alone claimed to have shot down fourteen of the enemy. [23]

By now the main German attack had developed against Tuxford's position. But the accurate and rapid fire of the Canadians broke up one rush after the other. Tuxford had the situation well in hand but he realized that if he stayed there much longer he would be outflanked and cut off.

Before dark the delicate process of disengagement took place, covered by mutual fire support, with the enemy pressing on close behind. On the way the Canadians passed by the trenches of the 3rd Royal Fusiliers, the left battalion of the adjacent 85th Brigade. Tuxford found that the Fusiliers had received no orders and were not conforming to the retirement. Thanks to the Fusiliers' covering fire the Canadians were able to reach their destination with only a few casualties. Later in the evening Tuxford and Lipsett took some of their men forward again to the Gravenstafel Ridge, remaining on the flank of the Fusiliers until relieved by the Hampshires at 3 AM on the 26th.[24]

On the left of the 2nd Brigade's front, the 7th and 10th Battalions did not receive the command to withdraw apparently because the messenger was killed. However the Canadians were in touch with the two Suffolk companies (on the crest between Boetleer Farm and Locality C) who had their orders and were preparing to move out. A meeting of the two senior Canadian officers in the line, Captain S.D. Gardner of the 7th and Major P.A. Guthrie of the 10th, led to a decision to remain until the Suffolks had completed their retirement. At dawn, under cover of mist, the two companies of Suffolk slipped out, followed by the remnants of the 7th and 10th Battalions. The Canadians reported to Brigade Headquarters near St. Jean while the Suffolks rejoined their battalion east of Fortuin.[25]

None of the units under Turner's command was heavily engaged on the 25th. But late in the afternoon Turner and some of his officers had a narrow brush with death. Here is what happened. Turner was studying a large map, in rear of his headquarters at Mouse Trap Farm, when an aeroplane circled twice overhead. The plane must have been German, even though it bore Allied markings, for within a few minutes incendiary shells came crashing in rapid succession on the farmhouse and the outbuildings that served as a dressing-station. The farmhouse caught fire, as did the straw on which the wounded were lying. Eventually the fire reached a dump of 200,000 rounds of rifle ammunition and the cartridges began to explode. The shelling continued and the whole place was filled with flames, Lyddite fumes and flying bullets. Through this inferno Captain Scrimger, assisted by a small band of devoted stretcher-bearers, calmly brought the wounded into the open.

The farm was surrounded by a moat, which was crossed by only one road. But the entrance across the moat was on the exposed side so that when Turner ordered the place evacuated all had to jump into the water and swim to safety. For Captain E.F. McDonald, a staff officer of the 3rd Brigade, swimming was out of the question. His wounds were so serious that no-one expected him to live. Scrimger carried him out of the blazing house and laid him down in a shallow ditch near the moat. He remained beside McDonald, coiling his body around the wounded officer's head and shoulder while shells exploded around them. Five shells fell within fifteen feet of the lying men, dazing them and half smothering them with flying mud. At length help arrived. Two of Turner's staff officers re-swam the moat and, waiting for a lull in the shelling, got the wounded man across the road on to a stretcher. For exceptional valour and devotion in succouring the wounded, Scrimger was awarded the Victoria Cross.[26]

During the past three days Alderson's force had been responsible for a five-mile fighting front, whereas the usual divisional sector averaged two miles, rarely more than three. Thus Plumer, on learning that the 11th British Brigade was at Vlamertinghe and the Lahore Division five miles southwest of Ypres, decided to reapportion the frontages in the northern face of the salient between Generals Alderson and Bulfin, GOC, 28th Division. His order, effective at 7 PM, reduced the Canadian sector to the two miles between Turco Farm and the Fortuin-St. Julien road and allocated to General

Bulfin the front and units east of the road as well as the fresh 11th Brigade. As soon as circumstances permitted units were to be sorted out and whenever possible returned to the brigades to which they belonged. The 2nd Canadian Brigade would be under the command of General Bulfin pending the 11th Brigade's arrival in the line. Such troops as could be spared were to be sent to Corps reserve at Potijze.[27]

After pondering Plumer's directive, Alderson issued orders at 6.15 PM for reorganization of his sector. General Hull was to hold the Corps flank from Fortuin to Mouse Trap Farm with his own brigade and the 1st Royal Irish. General Wanless O'Gowan was to replace Geddes' Detachment between Mouse Trap Farm and the French with the 13th Brigade, then in reserve west of the canal, and the 4th Rifle Brigade (27th Division). Geddes' four front-line battalions were to report to General Snow at Potijze but he was to remain at St. Jean with his three reserve battalions. The 149th Brigade was to serve as Alderson's reserve and assemble south of Wieltje. The 1st Canadian Brigade was to move back across the canal to take over control of the bridges from the 13th Brigade. Finally the 3rd Brigade was to bivouac at La Brique (southwest of St. Jean).[28]

The Germans, as usual, made no attacks during the night, permitting the movement and disentanglement of British units to commence. The 2nd Canadian Brigade, which was temporarily assigned to General Bulfin, departed from Wieltje on the morning of the 26th to occupy a position south of Fortuin. It remained in support of the 28th Division's left until after dark on the 27th when it crossed the canal into bivouac. By the time the three Canadian Brigades had gone into reserve, each had sustained about 1500 casualties.

The fighting around Ypres had taught the British that hasty, isolated attacks by the infantry alone could not stop the Germans from slicing off pieces of the front, much less expel them from the territory they had gained. Another offensive directed at the enemy was pointless unless carefully prepared, backed by sufficient artillery and in conjunction with a powerful effort by the French. The recent arrival of large reinforcements in the British and French sectors made it possible to mount the kind of operation that held some promise of success.

On the afternoon of 25 April an inter-Allied conference, at which Smith-Dorrien presided, agreed on a plan for combined action the following day. While the British pushed northwards on Langemarck, General Putz, with six divisions, would strike in three directions: General Joppé, adjoining the British troops, would attack from the east side of the canal toward Pilckem; as soon as Joppé's advance permitted, General Quiquandon would cross at Boesinghe and join the northward drive; on the left General Curé would aim to dislodge the Germans on the west bank at Lizerne, Steenstraat and Het Sas and then proceed in the direction of Bixschoote.[29]

That evening Smith-Dorrien drove to Hazebrouck where he was given Sir John's instructions in a personal interview. The Field Marshal indicated that he did not want to abandon any ground but that he might have to unless the French regained what they had lost or a good portion of it. He felt certain that the enemy's continuing attacks around Ypres were calculated to disrupt the projected Anglo-French offensive at Artois, which was then scheduled to start at the end of April. Determined to see that these plans were carried out, he wanted the situation cleared up and the area quieted as soon as possible even if it meant a further withdrawal. Sir John added irately that, as the French had got the Second Army into this difficulty, they ought to get it out. Nevertheless he approved of the British operation next day.

Smith-Dorrien had been led to believe that General Putz, now reinforced by three divisions, would employ sufficient troops to drive home his attack. At 10 PM when a copy of Putz's orders arrived at Second Army Headquarters it showed that he proposed to commit only one new division (less a brigade), together with those troops already in the line—a mere total of seventeen battalions. This news was followed by another French message saying that zero hour was to be moved up from 5 PM to 2 PM. Smith-Dorrien telephoned General Headquarters and protested first, that the French attack would not carry enough weight to have any effect and second, that advancing it three hours would curtail the already limited period available for preparations and for the rest needed by the Lahore Division (the troops detailed for the battle), which had marched all night. Sir John disregarded his objections and instructed him to proceed as arranged.

The objective of the Lahore Division was identical to that of Geddes' Detachment on 23 April, namely the German line between Kitchener's Wood and the Langemarck road. In several respects General Keary, who commanded the Indian Division, was better off than Geddes had been. He had a complete staff as had each of his two assaulting brigades, Ferozepore and Jullundur. He arrived at midday on the 25th and, having discussed matters with Smith-Dorrien, sent out his officers to arrange for artillery support and to see the roads, places of assembly and the ground over which the men were to advance. Thus he had time to gain useful information about his mission, make preparations and ensure that his orders reached all his units.

The Indian Division remained directly under the control of Smith-Dorrien whose operation orders called on the V Corps to launch an attack on its immediate right. In accordance with his instructions General Alderson directed the 149th (Northumberland) Brigade to attack St. Julien astride the Wieltje road and, at the same time, ordered the 10th Brigade to detail one battalion to advance between the two diverging forces. Geddes' three reserve battalions at St. Jean would move into the GHQ Line in support of the St. Julien attack. Canadian contribution to the operation was to be limited to a number of field batteries and the 3rd Brigade, placed

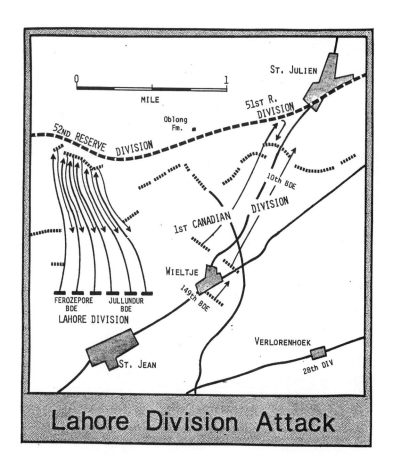

Lahore Division Attack

in divisional reserve south of Wieltje.

The attacking troops were more numerous but everything else favoured the enemy. The length of the British artillery barrage, fixed by the amount of ammunition available, was wholly insufficient to cut wire and flatten strong entrenchments. To make matters worse there was no time to lay lines to the observation officers and many of the batteries were too far from the front to zero in on their targets. The Germans, on the other hand, had enjoyed three days in which to improve their defences. They had a limitless amount of ammunition for their field batteries, the majority of which had been moved forward into the captured territory. Aided by excellent observation, both ground and air, German guns commanded every square inch of territory.

Around 12.30 PM the two assaulting brigades of the Lahore Division, each consisting of a British battalion and three Indian battalions, formed up side by side west of Wieltje. Straight ahead lay the ground where bitter fighting had taken place three days earlier. Like Geddes' Detachment, the Lahore Division had to march up Hill Top Ridge and then pass through a shallow valley before ascending the gentle slopes of Mauser Ridge.

About midday the long column of marching British and Indian soldiers had been spotted by enemy observation planes and heavy calibre shells from long-range guns began falling, causing casualties and disrupting the organization of the attacking lines. The fire continued, gradually rising in intensity and, as the leading waves of infantry raced down the reverse slope of Hill Top Ridge, German machine-guns joined in the action. Shells, particularly from 5.9-inch howitzers, landed with remarkable accuracy, knocking out entire platoons at a time. When the first of the attackers reached the bottom of the valley the ground behind was littered with bodies of the fallen. Several of the Indian battalions, their ranks badly depleted, broke up on losing all their British officers; some of the survivors remained crouched in shell holes while others turned and headed toward the old line. The British regulars on either flank, the 1st Manchesters and Connaught Rangers, gallantly pressed forward through the storm of machine-gun fire and the dark brown smoke from the shell bursts. Along with some Indian units they managed to reach the edge of the enemy's entanglements.

West of Langemarck General Joppé's attack had been launched punctually at 2 PM and at the outset some progress was made. Then at 2.20 PM the Germans played their trump card, releasing chlorine opposite the right French battalion. The wind, blowing from west to east, carried the gas across the front of the Lahore division. Without any means of protection the Indian battalions suffered heavily and the assault, which was faltering, now came to a dead stop. At night when the six front-line battalions were relieved by the Lahore Division's reserve brigade they had lost a total of 1829 of all ranks, including five battalion commanders.

On the extreme right the attack by the 149th Brigade (Northumberland Fusiliers) also fell short of its objective. Although the brigade was in reserve nearby at Wieltje, its commander, Brig.-Gen. J.F. Riddell, did not receive his orders to advance until 1.30 PM, 30 minutes before the chosen hour of the attack. Riddell got his men on the move before having had time to reconnoitre the area and with no more idea of what was required of him than the direction of the assault pointed out on a map. When the Fusiliers got through the narrow gap in the GHQ Line and deployed, they had missed what little artillery support there was. To further complicate matters Hull's 10th Brigade, instructed to connect the Fusiliers with the attack of the Lahore Division, was nowhere in sight. Hull's telephone lines had been cut by German bombardment and he received his orders too late to participate in the action.

Without artillery support the Fusiliers advanced over practically level ground where they were mowed down by

German machine-guns to the front and left. Riddell was himself killed after seeing hundreds of his men fall within a hundred yards of the British trenches. Although calls for reinforcements went unanswered there was no thought of retiring. Pinned in no man's land the men found shelter where they could and remained there until early next morning when they were ordered back to Wieltje. In its first engagement the brigade had lost 42 officers and 1912 other ranks—over two-thirds of its strength.[30]

Joppé's men wavered and in some places fell back on the appearance of the gas cloud but, as it blew diagonally, they pushed forward again. Enemy resistance stiffened when they came abreast of the Lahore Division and they went no further. Joppé's failure to gain the commanding ground on the east side of the canal prevented General Quiquandon from developing his attack against Boesinghe. French efforts on the west bank met with only limited results. Desperate fighting continued into the night and, although the French recovered parts of Het Sas and Lizerne, the Germans remained in possession of all of Steenstraat as well as their bridgeheads.[31]

A French staff report blamed their lack of success largely on the difficulties of command caused by placing newly arrived units and brigades under commanders who were unfamiliar with both their troops and the ground over which the advance was made.[32] Putz issued orders to pursue the offensive on the 27th and it was again arranged that the British left would co-operate. When Smith-Dorrien received a copy of Putz's orders[33] he was horrified that the weight of the French attack, upon which the whole operation depended, would be no greater than on the previous day. He at once dispatched a note to Putz, pointing out that the British troops were insufficient in numbers and too handicapped by their crammed position in the salient to achieve anything without substantial and effective French assistance. As a result of the British complaint, Putz directed General Joppé to employ his whole force.

To Smith-Dorrien the current policy of fragmentary attacks was both futile and costly. Experience had shown him that nothing but a carefully prepared and vigorous offensive could possibly expel the Germans from the ground they had gained and had been steadily fortifying for several days. No such effort could be contemplated in his sector. The French were organizing a great offensive in Artois and Sir John was committed to assist it. Any attempt to divert resources already limited for a big operation to regain the lost ground was likely to react adversely on the planned offensive further south. Yet to continue to attack without serious reinforcements was to invite failure and run the risk of heavy casualties.

During the morning of the 27th Smith-Dorrien forwarded to General Headquarters a summary of Putz's instructions, a copy of his own note and a reasoned assessment of the military situation in his sector. He did not expect that the operations of the day would advance the line and he went on to raise the question of possible withdrawal from the acute apex of the salient.[34] In reply Sir John indicated that he did not regard the situation nearly so unfavourably and, convinced there were ample troops and large reserves, ordered Smith-Dorrien to act vigorously in conjunction with the French.[35]

Smith-Dorrien again called on the Lahore Division to attack with two brigades east of Langemarck. The infantry assault was timed to start at 1.15 PM but it was understood that the Indian Brigades would leave their trenches only after the French advance had assured the safety of their left flank. The Indian Brigades, however, did not wait, moving forward at 12.30 PM in order to get the benefit of artillery cover. As on the previous day the attack withered away under heavy fire and was stopped well short of Mauser Ridge. The losses had been terrible. The Ferozepore Brigade alone was reduced to 38 officers and 1648 rifles.

Joppé's men, for their part, contributed absolutely nothing to the operation. They were pinned to the ground by a heavy barrage and never left their trenches. The only ray of encouragement occurred further north where General Curé completed the capture of Lizerne, taking 250 prisoners, and regained Het Sas and the line of the canal up to Steenstraat.

Toward the end of the afternoon Smith-Dorrien received an undeciphered message from General Headquarters, directing him to hand over the command of all the troops engaged around Ypres to General Plumer. Sir John, on the pretext that Smith-Dorrien had violated instructions, had chosen this time to settle old accounts.[36] Next morning at 7.50 French instructed Plumer to prepare for the very withdrawal that Smith-Dorrien had suggested. Three hours later the Field Marshal visited Foch at Cassel to inform him of his plans. He said that his troops were extremely tired, that the task of supplying them was becoming increasingly difficult and that he doubted he could continue to hold on to a tactically indefensible position. He did not wish to compromise the coming offensive at Arras by frittering away his reserves in secondary operations. But Foch rejected any notion of withdrawal, declaring that such a move would be an admission of weakness and would encourage the Germans to make fresh efforts to break through. He emphasized that the lost ground could be recaptured with the troops already available, adding that to win a second battle it was not necessary to lose a first. The upshot was that Sir John agreed to postpone his retirement pending the results of a major counter-attack, which was to be launched toward Langemarck on the 29th with the help of heavy artillery. In reporting the interview Foch told Joffre: 'I painted the picture of the consequences of withdrawal darker than they appeared to me.'[37]

Crisis had the effect of generating in Foch a kind of excitable euphoria. His prescription never varied, imbued as he was with the French pre-war doctrine of the offensive on all occasions. His buoyant assurances or flattering entreaties invariably overwhelmed Sir John who was nervous, inde-

174

cisive and subject to pressure. The scenes that followed behind the front could be likened to those of a comic opera if the consequences had not been so tragic. Day after day Sir John would learn of the absence of the much heralded French offensive and of the continued suffering of his men. Each time he would pass from optimism to pessimism, concluding that he must pull back his troops. And yet when confronted by the smooth-talking Foch he would swing the other way, agreeing to wait a little longer before withdrawing his men as well as to co-operate in one more counter-attack.

The French attacks on the afternoon of the 28th achieved little, mostly because Putz had insufficient means at his disposal. Curé's group overpowered the Germans in the wooded area between Het Sas and Lizerne but was stopped in front of Steenstraat. The remaining French forces laid down a heavy barrage on the enemy lines but did not advance. The Lahore Division, which had been told to move forward simultaneously with the French, did not stir either. A staff officer's report to Joffre, summarizing the day's events, ended by saying:

> General Foch is very calm and very confident. But he does not want to call up other troops for he estimates that for the moment he has enough for his front. He is going to try to convince Field Marshal French of the necessity of the English making a violent effort to re-establish the situation.[38]

As part of a consolidation plan General Plumer had instructed Alderson to close the gap between the French and British.[39] Accordingly four Canadian battalions were detailed for the trench-digging job. The troops trudged forward in the moonlit night, passing over the bodies of scores of Gurkhas who had fallen under the bursts of fire that morning. With the 2nd Battalion acting as a covering party, the rest began digging along the line marked by the engineers.

Judging from the multitude of flares and the persistence of sniper bullets, which mercifully passed overhead, the Germans must have known what was taking place. For men 'not yet recovered from their gruelling experiences of the past few days, it was a nerve-racking job.'[40] The task was completed around 2.15 AM on the 29th, to the delight of the men who marched back wearily to their billets in the Vlamertinghe-Elverdinghe area. A 1200-yard stretch of ground between Hampshire and Turco Farms had been gained without a casualty. Nevertheless one must question the wisdom of occupying a 1200-yard stretch of overlooked ground. This was the kind of daft tactics that caused so many casualties.

The French assault planned for the 29th was postponed until next day to allow the newly arrived artillery time to register. Sir John at once consented to maintain his troops in their forward position another day. The allied operations on the 30th were hampered by fog and the French made only small local attacks. In the evening Foch motored to Hazebrouck and at his urgent representations Sir John agreed to delay the British withdrawal for yet another 24 hours. Putz, under pressure from Foch, ordered the attack renewed on 1 May, but when the hour came his men refused to leave their trenches. Later in the day Foch visited Sir John but this time he was not seeking a further delay. He had in his possession a telegram from Joffre ordering him to 'act on the defensive about Ypres' and to conserve all resources for the projected attack on the Arras front. Sir John welcomed the news and it was agreed that the British should withdraw from the tip of the salient, the evacuation to commence that evening with the troops not required for defence. The movement was carried out without a hitch during the night of 1-2 May.

On the afternoon of 2 May, before the next stage of the retirement could take place, a shift in the wind enabled the Germans to launch a gas attack on a three-mile front between St. Julien and Berlin Wood. The area was defended by three brigades of the 4th Division—the newly arrived 12th Bri-

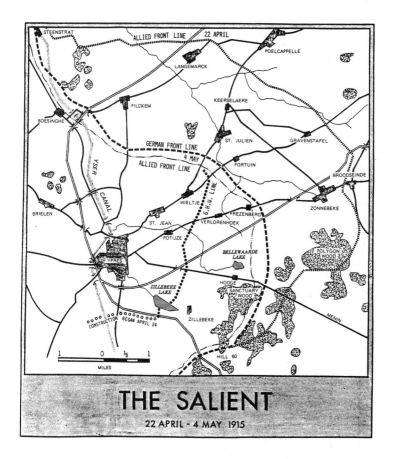

THE SALIENT
22 APRIL - 4 MAY 1915

gade and the remains of the 10th and 11th—all under the command of General Alderson. Fortunately for the British their trenches here were far apart and the fitful wind distributed the gas unevenly. As a result the poisonous fumes lacked the density to overwhelm the defenders although every man was more or less affected. In some places the troops in the trenches drew to one side to avoid the gas; in others they waited for the oncoming cloud of vapour and charged swiftly through it, falling with the bayonet on the Germans behind it. At the end of the day's fighting the Germans had only gained two lengths of trench west of Mouse Trap Farm. On the first alarm the Canadian Brigades were alerted, but, as it turned out, were not required.

The Germans renewed the assault next day, concentrating near the junction of the 11th and 85th Brigades at Berlin Wood. The British had to rely mainly on rifle fire since all but three field batteries had been withdrawn from the area. Several units were badly mauled but reinforcements were rushed up through the shelled zone in time to stop the enemy's advance.

When the fighting died down the 85th and 11th Brigades were in such close contact with the enemy that in places they were separated by only a few yards. Nevertheless it was decided to proceed with the planned withdrawal of the 27th and 28th Divisions and the right of the Canadian Division. On the night of 3-4 May the movement was carried out, in perfect order and without the loss of a man. The new line ran from Turco Farm, curved around Frezenberg and, continuing in a southerly direction, passed in front of Hooge and along the eastern fringes of Sanctuary Wood before rejoining the old front, half a mile north-east of Hill 60.[41] This line was about three miles shorter than the old one and so, with fewer troops needed to hold it, some of the brigades, which had been most sorely tired, were given a chance to rest.

At 10 AM on 4 May Alderson handed over his front to General H.F.M. Wilson, GOC 4th Division. The Canadian

Divisional Artillery remained in position attached to the 4th Division and covering the front between Mouse Trap and Turco Farms. The remaining units of the Canadian Division, after as trying an initiation in battle as any troops ever received, retired to the Bailleul area for a well deserved rest.

EPILOGUE

The Second Battle of Ypres continued, almost without abatement, for another three weeks. Some British units suffered appalling losses, more heavily than even the Canadians. It seemed as if the Germans, suddenly realizing how close they had come to achieving their goal, were making frantic efforts to recover the opportunity they had lost.

The only Canadian battalion engaged in the later phase of the Battle was the Princess Patricia's Canadian Light Infantry, which had crossed to France as part of the 80th Brigade of the 27th Division. From 7 January to 23 March the Patricias served in the St. Eloi sector where they garrisoned the line, conducted several daring raids and took part in a small local attack. In the first ten weeks of trench warfare the unit sustained 238 battle casualties, among them its brilliant and fearless commander, Lt.-Col. F.D. Farquhar. [1]

The Patricias entered the Ypres salient on 5 April when the 27th Division relieved the French 17th Division. Four days later they occupied 700 yards of front along the southern edge of Polygon Wood, about three miles south of the 2nd Canadian Brigades's right at Berlin Wood. The area was relatively quiet for the first two weeks but after the fighting began on the northern flank the battalion was under constant shell fire and took 80 casualties. [2] When the withdrawal occurred during the night of 3-4 May the Patricias established a defensive position on Bellewaarde Ridge, a small hill to the east of Ypres. The Germans were quick to follow up, pushing machine-guns to within 200 yards and ranging their field guns on the new trenches. In their unfinished, shallow trenches the Patricias suffered 122 casualties before the enemy's fire subsided that evening. Next morning the CO Lt.-Col. H.C. Buller was struck in the eye by a shrapnel fragment and invalided to England. Major A. Hamilton Gault, who had just returned to duty after being wounded in the forearm, assumed command of the battalion.

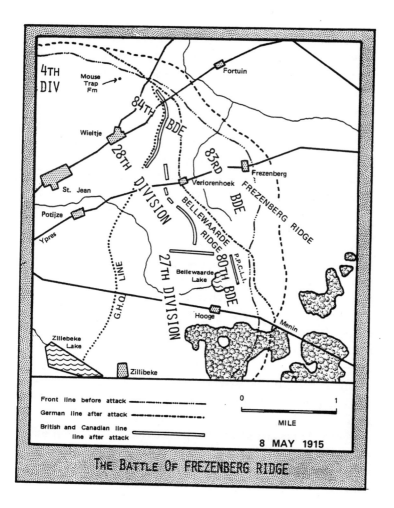

4TH DIV

Mouse Trap Fm →

Fortuin

84TH BDE

Wieltje

28TH DIVISION

83RD BDE

St. Jean

Verlorenhoek

Frezenberg

FREZENBERG RIDGE

Potijze

BELLEWAARDE RIDGE

Ypres

G.H.Q. LINE

27TH DIVISION

P.P.C.L.I.

80TH BDE

Bellewaarde Lake

Hooge

Menin

Zillebeke Lake

Zillibeke

Front line before attack	—··—··—
German line after attack	—·—·—·—·—
British and Canadian line line after attack	▬▬▬

0   1

MILE

8 MAY 1915

THE BATTLE OF FREZENBERG RIDGE

Encouraged by the British withdrawal from the apex, the Duke of Albrecht made another determined effort to reduce the salient. On 6 May he issued orders for converging attacks by three corps of the German Fourth Army: the XVth Corps was to break north-westward between Zillebeke and Bellewaarde Lakes; the XXVIth Reserve Corps in the centre was to carry out the initial and main thrust westward against the Bellewaarde Lake to Frezenberg sector; and the XXVIIth Reserve Corps was to advance from the north, between Frezenberg and Mouse Trap Farm, with the object of gaining the high ground about Wieltje. The operation was set to begin at 7 AM on 8 May.[3]

As a preliminary move Albrecht had ordered the capture of Hill 60 at the south-western extremity of the salient. On the morning of 5 May troops of the 30th Division followed behind a cloud of gas, which drifted over the British trenches where most of the garrison, except for the usual guards, were asleep. In very bitter fighting the Germans gained the top of the hill and then withstood repeated attempts by the British to recover it.[4]

The silence in the early hours of daylight on the 8th was shattered by a violent artillery bombardment, which transcended anything the British had experienced before. Along the entire front of the Vth Corps, huge projectiles fell with relentless precision, obliterating whole stretches of trenches and burying occupants. When the guns lifted two and a half hours later, masses of German infantrymen swarmed out of their trenches.

The weight of the main attack was directed at the exposed front of Frezenberg Ridge, which was held by the 83rd Brigade of the 28th Division. Driven back twice, the Germans broke through on the third attempt, capturing Frezenberg and penetrating as far as Verlorenhoek. They advanced no further, possibly because of increasing British resistance. By mid-afternoon the Germans, having widened the breach in the salient to two miles, proceeded to roll up the line of the

84th and 80th Brigades on either flank.

The Patricias were deployed on Bellewaarde Ridge, forming the extreme left flank of the 80th Brigade with the 4th King's Royal Rifle Corps on their right. The storm of shells that the enemy concentrated on the British line from the Menin Road to Frezenberg blew in the Patricias' trenches, put out of action two of their four machine-guns and smashed the wire in front. Casualties came so fast that Major Gault ordered support personnel—orderlies, pioneers, signallers, batmen—into the secondary line. Though their numbers had been thinned the defenders brought a deadly fire to bear, stopping the enemy's initial on-rush. The Germans kept up the pressure, mounting a major assault at 9 AM, which was preceded by a tremendous artillery barrage. The trenches of No. 1 Company (under Captain H.S. Dennison) on the right were obliterated and became untenable. Consequently Dennison sent back the remnant of his company while he stayed behind with a handful of men to cover the withdrawal.

The results of the second German attack were mixed. On the left the steady fire of No. 2 Company drove them back but on the right they gained a foothold when they overpowered Dennison and his little band. The men of No. 2 Company could now be enfiladed but they remained in position and kept up a hot and effective fire on the enemy trying to close in. Finally, with their ammunition nearly expended and the knowledge that both their flanks were being turned, they carried out a successful and daring retirement along the shallow communication trench.[5]

By 10 AM the battalion, save for a few isolated outposts in the front trenches, occupied the support line on the crest. Here the Patricias endured a devastating bombardment, punctuated only when the enemy's infantry attempted to advance from the captured trenches. Major Gault and all the senior officers were killed or wounded and the command devolved upon Lieutenant H.W. Niven, who refused to obey orders to withdraw. In later life Niven gave the following explanation:

> I had been told to retire, that the 27th Division couldn't help me, that they couldn't get up to me and they couldn't give me any support, and it was just madness to stay there, and I wrote back and said that I had too many wounded. We had no stretcher bearers to take out the wounded and I wouldn't go and leave them. So then they sent for me and I had to go back, about ... a mile, to talk to the Divisional Commander and tell him that I wouldn't go back. I couldn't retire. I was only a lieutenant but no general in the British Army could make me go back without what was left.[6]

Thus the Patricias stood unflinchingly for the rest of the day. Around noon a company of the 4th Rifle Brigade gallantly pushed forward through the raging inferno with boxes of ammunition and two machine-guns. The men were posted on the left where the remnants of the 83rd Brigade's two right battalions, cut off when the Germans broke through the centre, continued to fight from isolated positions. Later in the afternoon the left flank was extended by reserve battalions of the 80th and 81st Brigades, which joined with counter-attacking battalions of the 85th Brigade to seal off the gap.

Pressure on the Patricias' front eased by 4 PM when the Germans became occupied with the 85th Brigade counter-attack, which turned the tide that day. When the Patricias were relieved shortly before midnight their strength had been reduced to 4 officers and 150 men. The recorded casualties of the battalion for the day were 392 all ranks. General Snow, the Divisional Commander, paid generous tribute to the contribution of the Patricias in his report: 'No regiment could have fought with greater determination or endurance, many would have failed where they succeeded.'[7]

The Patricias were not called upon to go into the front line again during the remainder of the fighting around Ypres, which died down out of pure exhaustion in the last week of May. The Germans made a last ditch effort to reach Ypres on the 24th. On a front of over four miles they released a heavy concentration of chlorine, followed by an infantry assault. However, the British troops had been issued makeshift respirators, which shielded their lungs from the strangling poison. When the Germans advanced they met unexpected resistance and in many places were driven back to their trenches by the blazing fire. The Germans captured Mouse Trap Farm and Bellewaarde Ridge but that was the extent of their gains. The opposing lines around Ypres would remain practically unchanged until the summer of 1917.

For its size Second Ypres was one of the deadliest clashes of the war. Aggregate British losses amounted to 60,000 men, or nearly twice the German total of 35,000. It was one of the rare instances in the war in which the defenders suffered considerably heavier casualties than did the attackers.

Second Ypres was a new kind of battle in that materials were matched against men. The Germans' superiority in guns was somewhere in the proportion of six to one and they seemed to have at their disposal an unlimited supply of shells. In their anxiety to spare their infantry they turned to their overwhelming artillery and, whenever possible, discharges of gas, to sweep away the defenders. On the other hand British troops were frequently compelled to rely almost solely on their rifles in their efforts to stop the enemy's steady encroachment. If the British leaders learned one lesson from Second Ypres it was that they needed many more heavy guns to match or counter the enemy's fire. Never again during the war were British infantrymen called upon to maintain so protracted or so unequal a struggle.

Had the Allied generals paid closer attention to repeated warnings that the Germans intended to use gas, it is possible that the fighting at Ypres would not have developed into a major battle. The evidence, coming as it did from different sources, was strong enough to require that the troops be told.

At the time little could be done in the way of counteracting the effect of the chlorine, but forewarning would have reduced the psychological terror of the unknown and, perhaps, prevented the panic and rout that ensued.

One may well ask what the Allies were doing in the salient in the first place? The primary reason given for its retention was emotional, not strategic. The French, as well as many British generals, felt that the occupation of additional Belgian territory by the rampaging German armies would impair the morale of their troops. But this is specious reasoning. Normally strategic retreats do not have an adverse effect on trained soldiers, as was shown in 1917, when the Germans fought, if anything, better after the great withdrawal to the Hindenburg line. Another argument frequently heard was that the salient was an admirable spring-board for an allied offensive to roll up the German left flank. In fact it was so used in the second half of 1917 at the Third Battle of Ypres (popularly called Passchendaele) but the less said about the disastrous results of that battle the better. Finally it was claimed that the salient stood directly at the crossroads to the Channel ports of Dunkirk, Calais and Boulogne, and that the loss of Ypres would make it difficult for Britain to send supplies and reinforcements to the Western front. However, any German advance in the direction of the Channel ports could have been blunted more easily several miles further back where the defenders could have held a shorter and stronger line.

If the Allies, in defiance of military logic, were determined to hold on to the salient, they should at least have prepared a new line in the rear to which they could fall back in the event of a serious attack. At any rate after the two French divisions had fled the British should have exerted every effort during one of the periodic lulls to withdraw to a defensive position outside Ypres. On no account should they have tried to defend what remained of the salient, which was even more vulnerable to enemy artillery than it had originally been.

The manner in which the British High Command managed the battle exacerbated the difficulties for the men in the field. Beginning with the first gas attack, Plumer can be criticized for making no change of divisional boundaries and leaving Alderson to cope with a five-mile gap in the line. The 28th Division enjoyed relative quiet and an extension of that unit's front to include the Gravenstafel-St. Julien sector would have divided the load. It would have greatly facilitated command and supply; and reduced confusion by negating the need to place the Corps reserve in the hands of General Snow (GCO 27th Division), a soldier who was unfamiliar with the disposition of the troops there, the sector under attack and the brigade commanders fighting in the line.

There were two viable options to counter siege warfare tactics as practised by the Germans at Ypres. The first was a quick sortie, to strike before the enemy had time to fortify his new position. The other was a deliberately prepared attack, requiring proper reconnaissance, adequate numbers and carefully arranged artillery co-operation. In the operations at Ypres Sir John allowed the choice to be taken out of his hands when he bound himself to French plans and wishes.

Foch led Sir John to believe that British action would merely entail assisting the French in recapturing the ground they had lost. The little Frenchman acted in bad faith for he really never tried to uphold his end of the bargain. Admittedly he issued orders for counter-attacks but General Putz did not have the means to execute them and rarely budged. At no time did Foch insist that his commander employ his full strength. The plain truth was that Foch quickly realized that restoration of the line by French local reserves was tactically impossible. As he had no intentions of compromising the projected Arras offensive by calling up large reinforcements, he cajoled and deceived Sir John into carrying most of the burden. Discussing Foch's behaviour, Gordon-Hall wrote with some acerbity:

He gained his point by deceiving Sir J. French at little loss of his own troops, but at a cost of confidence comparable to the early days of the war when the British Army felt that the French did not play the game, but were ready to sacrifice the British whenever pressed. This lost confidence was never restored, but rather increased and the war prolonged. History will not exonerate Foch.[8]

Again and again French pledges to co-operate failed to materialize and British counter-attacks continued alone, in a vain cause. All these counter-attacks, save for the Canadian night assault on Kitchener's Wood, were operationally unsound. None could be considered as true deliberate counter-attacks. Reconnaissance was inadequate, objectives were unrealistic, the routes chosen were dangerous, frequently suicidal, and, worst of all, there was not even the amount of artillery support that pre-war teaching would have regarded as necessary, let alone what recent experience had shown to be indispensible. Commanders have the right to demand the maximum from their men, but not the impossible. At Second Ypres the impossible was demanded over and over again with predictably grievous losses. Indeed, had it not been for the heavy casualties incurred in the initial counter-attacks and then in the assaults on the 23rd, a decent flank could have been formed and the disasters of the following days might never have occurred.

As for the Canadian Command, Alderson and his staff were generally unable to influence the course of events in view of their limited authority in defining objectives, the dearth of information and the unusual battle conditions. They could not do much more than pass on Corps instructions for counter-attacks to be made and distribute what reinforcements were available, leaving the commanders on the spot to deal with the situation as it developed.

At the brigade level and below nearly all the Canadian officers were amateur soldiers. This proved to be a benefit in some instances, a handicap in others. Overall the Canadians committed few grave errors. It is difficult to conceive of a worse choice than the close-order formation adopted for the attack on Kitchener's Wood. In defence of the two Canadian battalions it should be mentioned that they had learned no other method of conducting a night assault.

Then too, there were serious flaws in Turner's staff work and tactical moves on the 24th. He was never certain of the position of his front line and throughout the day sent conflicting reports of its location to Divisional Headquarters. Less excusable was his panic withdrawal to the GHQ Line, which caused not only additional suffering to his own men but the near distruction of the Second Brigade.

Balancing these mistakes was Currie's magnificent response to the enemy's break-in at the apex. He quickly formed an accurate picture of what was happening and, considering the gravity of the situation, exercised remarkable control over his brigade. He possessed sound tactical judgment and did not hesitate when committing his reserves, an action that enabled the 2nd Brigade to maintain its position longer than anyone had the right to expect. Some, including myself, believe that Currie ought not to have left his command post but at least he displayed boldness in going back for more reinforcements when other means failed. Finally his decision to hold Locality C as vital ground promoted the idea of all-round, as opposed to linear, defence. This concept was refined, regrettably not by the Allies but by Ludendorff and Hindenburg in the autumn of 1917.

It has often been said that the Germans committed the most serious blunder of the war through their premature and local use of poison gas. Properly exploited, the new weapon might have permitted the Germans to break the deadlock of trench warfare and win the war in the west. They missed an opportunity that would not come again, except in March 1918. In the long run the introduction of poison gas did the Germans more harm than good. It laid them open to heavy reprisals because the prevailing winds were westerly. No less important was the damage that it did to Germany's reputation in the neutralist countries, particularly in the United States where indignation was to be further fuelled by the sinking of the *Lusitania* on 7 May.

German unwillingness to appreciate the potentiality of the new weapon led to a series of miscalculations at the outset of the battle: no follow-up plan had been prepared; there were insufficient reserves to exploit the initial success; the objectives were too limited; and the attack on the 22nd even if pressed with enough determination, which it was not, was launched too late in the day to permit sweeping gains before last light. Still, the Germans quickly recognized their errors and, taking corrective measures when possible, fought reasonably well during the remainder of Second Ypres. If their attack on the 22nd had been as carefully planned and executed as the one made two days later, it is almost certain that the salient would have fallen into their hands.

Yet when everything has been said it remains true that the principal reason for the German failure had been the presence of three Canadian Brigades composed of men accustomed to civilian life—lawyers, college professors, graduates, labourers, farmers and clerks—and who, in thousands of cases, had never handled a gun before rallying to their country's call. During the crucial first three days of battle these ill-equipped and untried amateur soldiers had held the vital left flank of the Second British Army against superior artillery and many times their numbers, and had not broken even under the horrible surprise of poison gas. By 25 April enough British and French reinforcements had arrived to end the danger of a German break-through.

If the Canadian troops had been a little more experienced, or a little less, they might not have responded so gallantly to official policy to hold the line 'at all costs'; and they might not have taken so literally the order that 'ground once lost must be retaken' and counter-attacked with such reckless valour. By their tenacious stand they had undoubtedly saved a quarter of the British front-line forces in France from being cut off and destroyed. Moreover, they had robbed the Germans of a decisive victory that could have changed the course of the entire war.

A steady stream of messages from all over the world poured into Ottawa, carrying ringing words of praise for Canada's soldiers. The bearing and conduct of the Canadian troops, Sir John French reported in his dispatch, 'had averted a disaster, which might have been attended with the most serious consequences.'[9] General Alderson, in addressing his men, was no less generous:

> I would, first of all, tell you that I have never been so proud of anything in my life as I am of this armlet with 'Canada' on it.... I thank you, and congratulate you from the bottom of my heart, for the part each one of you have taken in giving me this feeling of pride.
>
> I think it is possible that you do not, all of you, quite realize that, if we had retired on the evening of 22 April— when our Allies fell back before the gas and left our left flank quite open—the whole of the 27th and 28th Divisions would probably have been cut off.... My lads, if ever men had a right to be proud in this world, you have.
>
> I know my military history pretty well, and I cannot think of an instance, especially when the cleverness and determination of the enemy is taken into account, in which troops were placed in such a difficult position; nor can I think of an instance in which so much depended on the standing fast of one Division.
>
> You will remember that the last time I spoke to you, just before you went into the trenches ... now over two months ago, I told you about my old regiment—the Royal West Kents—having gained a reputation for not budging from their trenches, no matter how they were attacked. I said then I was quite sure that, in a short time, the Army

out here would be saying the same of you.

I little thought—none of us thought—how soon those words would come true. But now, today, not only the Army out here, but all Canada, all England and all the Empire are saying it of you. [10]

In their baptism of fire the men and officers of the 1st Canadian Division learned that they could bear comparison with any other troops, allied or enemy. Had they not stood fast when the French fled? Had they not, under very trying circumstances, proven themselves more than a match for the enemy? The Second Battle of Ypres, tragic though it was, gave the Canadians an indomitable confidence that was to carry them irresistibly forward throughout the remainder of the war.

The casualties of the 1st Canadian Division from 22 April to 3 May had been appalling, even when judged by the standards of the Great War. Out of a front-line infantry strength of some 10,000, the number of killed, wounded and missing totalled 6037—208 officers and 5829 other ranks. The infantry losses were almost equally distributed among the three brigades with 1839 for the 1st, 1829 for the 2nd and 1838 for the 3rd. [11]

Canada, in grateful remembrance of her sons' suffering and sacrifice at the Second Battle of Ypres, erected a memorial that was formally unveiled by the Duke of Connaught, a former Governor-General, on 8 July, 1923. The moving and impressive ceremony was attended by such illuminaries as the Belgian Crown Prince, Marshal Foch and Sir John French. The monument was designed by Frederick Clemesha of Regina who supervised its construction at the Keerselaere crossroads, one mile north of the rebuilt town of St. Julien. It consists of a single giant shaft of flagstone court, on which is surmounted the head and shoulders of a Canadian soldier. His hands are folded, resting on a reversed rifle and, under a steel helmet, his head is bowed in perpetual tribute to those who fell. On the front of the plinth is inscribed the word 'Canada' and on each side—one in English and the other in French—is the bare statement:

This column marks the battlefield where 18,000 Canadians on the British left withstood the First German Gas Attack the 22nd—24th April, 1915. Two thousand fell and lie buried here.

Actually the Canadians who perished at Ypres are not buried in the memorial plot but may be found in the many British cemeteries in the area. The names of those whose bodies were never recovered are inscribed, as are other Canadians who suffered a similar fate in different battles in Belgium, on the Menin Gate Memorial. Many of those who could not be identified lie in British cemeteries. On their headstone is the insignia of a maple leaf, or regimental crest if known, with the inscription 'Known Unto God.'

The site of the St. Julien memorial, once bare and closely pitted with the shell holes, is beautifully landscaped. Groupings of shrubs and beds of juniper, roses and Canadian wildflowers beneath the trees are painstakingly shaped to compliment the towering shaft and the mourning soldier.

There is another Canadian memorial commemorating the soldiers at Ypres for whom the Last Post had sounded—one that may outlast even the monument of stone. During the battle John McCrae, a medical officer with the 1st Canadian Field Artillery Brigade, wrote what was to become perhaps the best known poem of the Great War.

Born in Guelph, Ontario, in 1872, McCrae studied medicine at the University of Toronto, earning a BM in 1898. Interrupting his medical career, he volunteered for the South African War as an artillery subaltern. In 1900 he returned to Canada whereupon he was appointed Fellow in pathology at McGill University and Pathologist at the Montreal General Hospital. He became a physician of some note and authored a number of medical texts. In his idle moments he wrote poetry and occasionally contributed verses to the *University Magazine* and other periodicals. When the country rallied to arms in August 1914, McCrae, although a gunner at heart, joined the medical corps where he felt he could best contribute.

At the time that the Germans launched their gas attack, McCrae was in charge of a dressing-station dug into a bank somewhere behind the Yser Canal. Working practically around the clock he agonized over the suffering of the wounded and the rapidly growing number of little wooden crosses. One evening, as he sat quietly at a table, there came to him words that he hastily scribbled down on a piece of paper. Shortly he raised his head and his close friend, Lt.-Col. E.W.B. Morrison, CO of the 1st Brigade, Canadian Field Artillery, asked him to read what he had written. McCrae did so diffidently. Believing the poem to be worthless, he crushed the paper up in a ball and threw it into the waste-basket. Morrison, who in private life was the editor of the *Ottawa Citizen,* recognized the artistic merits of the poem and immediately retrieved it. He later sent it to *Punch* magazine.[12] The poem, entitled 'In Flanders Fields,' came out in the issue of 8 December, 1915. The best note on which to leave 'Second Ypres' is to savour the exquisite form and beauty of McCrae's rondeau:

In Flanders fields the poppies blow
Between the crosses, row on row,
That mark our place; and in the sky
The larks, still bravely singing, fly
Scarce heard amid the guns below.

We are the Dead. Short days ago
We lived, felt dawn, saw sunset glow,
Loved and were loved, and now we lie
    In Flanders fields.

Take up our quarrel with the foe:
To you from failing hands we throw
The torch; be yours to hold it high.
If ye break faith with us who die
We shall not sleep, though poppies grow
   In Flanders fields.

NOTES

TRAINING THE CEF

1 Robert Laird Borden, *His Memoirs* (New York, 1938), vol. I, pp. 452-53.

2 Harcourt (Secretary for the Colonies) to Duke of Connaught (Governor General), 6 August, 1914; Appendix 42 to General Staff, Historical Section, *The Canadian Forces in the Great War, 1914-1919* (Ottawa, 1938), vol. I. This work includes copies of original documents designed to reinforce and elaborate upon the first volume of Col. A. Fortescue Duguid's official history.

3 Oscar Douglas Skelton, *Life and Letters of Sir Wilfred Laurier* (New York, 1922), vol. II, pp. 432-33.

4 Elizabeth H. Armstrong, *The Crisis of Quebec* (New York, 1937), pp. 55-56.

5 Sir Charles Lucas, *The Empire At War* (London, 1923), vol. II, p. 82.

6 Col. A. Fortescue Duguid, *The Canadian Forces in the Great War, 1914-1919* (Ottawa, 1938), vol. I, pp. 97-98; G.F.C. Stanley, *Canada's Soldiers, 1604-1954* (Toronto, 1954), p. 310.

7 'Note on the Overseas Mobilization Scheme 1911-1912,' Appendix 11.

8 Minister of Militia to Officers Commanding Divisions and Districts, 6 August, 1914, Appendix 44.

9 Duguid, op. cit., vol. I, pp. 26-28.

10 House of Commons, *Debates,* 26 January, 1916, vol. I, p. 292.

11 'Report on the State of the Militia of the Province of Canada for 1865-66,' Appendix 52.

12 John Swettenham, *To Sieze the Victory* (Toronto, 1965), pp. 31-32.

13 Col. George G. Nasmith, *Canada's Sons and Great Britain in the World War* (Toronto, 1919), pp. 80-81.

14 Stanley, op. cit., p. 311.

15 Jeffrey Williams, *Princess Patricia's Canadian Light Infantry* (London, 1972), pp. 1-5.

16 Borden, op. cit., vol. I, pp. 464-65.

17 Col. G.W.L. Nicholson, *Official History of the Canadian Army in the First World War: Canadian Expeditionary Force, 1914-1919* (Ottawa, 1962), p. 22.

18 Swettenham, op cit., pp. 30-31.

19 Borden to Perley, 14 August, 1914; MG27 II D12, vol. I, Perley papers.

20 Kitchener to Perley, 16 August, 1914 (ibid).

21 Borden to Perley, 29, August 1914 (ibid); Desmond Morton, 'Exerting Control: The Development of Canadian Authority Over the Canadian Expeditionary Force, 1914-1919,' p. 12, in Timothy Travers and Christon Archer, eds., *Men At War* (Chicago, 1982).

22 Kitchener to Perley, 5 September, 1914; MG27 II D12, vol. I, Perley papers.

23 Nicholson, op. cit., p. 34.

24 Duguid, op. cit., vol. I, pp. 126-27.

25 Brig.-Gen. Charles F. Winter, *The Hon. Sir Sam Hughes* (Toronto, 1931), p. 53.

26 Kitchener was convinced that the war would last at least three years.

27 Nicholson, op. cit., p. 23.

28 Lucas, op. cit., vol. I, pp. 83-84.

29 A.J. Gorrie to Price, 6 October, 1914, Appendix 130.

30 Kirkpatrick diary, 15 October, 1914; MG30 E318, vol. 23, file 179, Official records.

31 Duguid, op. cit., Vol. I, p. 119.

32 Kirkpatrick diary, 12 November, 1914; MG30 E318, Vol. 23, file 179, Official records.

33 Hugh M. Urquhart, *The History of the 16th Battalion (Canadian Scottish) in the Great War, 1914-1919* (Toronto, 1932), pp. 30-31.

34 Duguid, op. cit., vol. I, p. 136.

35 Kirkpatrick diary, 30 November, 1914; MG30 E318, vol. 23, file 179, Official records.

36 Nicholson, op. cit., p. 26.

37 'The Ross Rifle,' Appendix 111.

38 Cited in Nicholson, op. cit., p. 38.

39 Creelman diary, 19 December, 1914; MG30 E8, Creelman papers.

40 Col. J.A. Currie, *The Red Watch: With the First Canadian Division in Flanders* (Toronto, 1916), pp. 84-85.

41 Ralph Hodder Williams, *Princess Patricia's Canadian Light Infantry, 1914-1919* (Toronto, 1923), vol. I, pp. 14-17.

42 Currie, op. cit., pp. 98-99.

[1] Urquhart, *History of the 16th Battalion,* p. 41.

[2] Duguid, op. cit., vol. I, pp. 172-73.

[3] Cited in Ibid., p. 173.

[4] French diary, 20 February, 1915, French papers (Imperial War Museum, London).

[5] On the Schlieffen Plan see especially Gerhard Ritter, *The Schlieffen Plan* (London, 1958), and L.C.F. Turner, 'The Signigicance of the Schlieffen Plan,' in Paul M. Kennedy ed., *The War Plans of the Great Powers, 1880-1914* (London 1979). Von Moltke was subsequently blamed for the failure of the plan because of his unwillingness to adhere strictly to his predecessor's recommendation. Recent studies, however, have shown that the plan was not likely to succeed under the best of circumstances. The cause of the German defeat may be summarized as a disproportion between the high aims of the Schlieffen Plan and existing German military strength.

[6] On Plan XVII see especially S.R. Williamson, 'Joffre reshapes French Strategy' in *War Plans of the Great Powers,* Barbara Tuchman, *The Guns of August* (New York, 1962), Ch. 3; and Paul Marie de la Gorce, *The French Army* (New York, 1963), Ch. 5.

[7] For a detailed treatment of the opening moves see Tuchman, op. cit.; and General Staff, Historical Section, *The Western Front, 1914* (Ottawa, 1957).

[8] Brig.-Gen. Sir James E. Edmonds, *Official History of the Great War. Military Operations. France and Belgium, 1915* (London, 1927), vol. I, p. 69.

[9] 'Address by General Alderson,' Appendix 267.

[10] Duguid, op. cit., vol. I, p. 157.

[11] Mercer, then in command of the 3rd Canadian Division, was killed by a burst of shrapnel during fighting at Mount Sorrel in the Ypres salient in June 1916.

[12] The best study of Currie is A.M.J. Hyatt, 'The Military Career of Sir Arthur Currie,' Duke University Ph.D. thesis, 1965.

[13] 'Principles of Defence,' 4 March, 1915, Appendix 270.

[14] Edmonds, *France and Belgium, 1915,* vol. I, pp. 66-69.

[15] George H. Cassar, *The Tragedy of Sir John French* (Cranbury, 1985), pp. 205-10.

[16] On British tactics during the war see Dominick Graham, 'Sans Doctrine:

British Army Tactics in the First World War,' in *Men At War*; and Shelford Bidwell and Dominick Graham, *Firepower: British Army Weapons and Theories of War 1904-1945* (London, 1982).

17 Bidwell and Graham, op. cit., p. 3.

18 There are many accounts on the Battale of Neuve Chapelle but among the most perceptive are Graham, op. cit., pp. 79-80; and Bidwell and Graham, op. cit., pp. 73-77.

19 'Memorandum on Training,' 26 March 1915, Appendix 306.

20 Cassar, op. cit., pp. 216-20.

21 First Army to 1st Can. Div., 1 April, 1915, Appendix 306a.

22 During the South African War Smith-Dorrien commanded the 19th Brigade which included the 2nd Battalion, Royal Canadian Regiment.

23 'Smith-Dorrien's address to the Canadian troops,' Smith-Dorrien papers; Hugh M. Urquhart, *Arthur Currie: The Biography of a Great Canadian* (Toronto, 1950), pp. 58-59.

UNHEEDED WARNING

1 Edmonds, *France and Belgium, 1914,* vol. II, Chs. V-XVII; Cassar, op. cit., pp. 165-78; Gen. Sir James Marshall-Cornwall, *Haig as Military Commander* (New York, 1973), Ch. 9.

2 Hugh B.C. Pollard, *The Story of Ypres* (New York, 1917), p. 65.

3 John Giles, *The Ypres Salient* (London, 1970), p. 31.

4 Pollard, op. cit., pp. 14-15.

5 Ibid., pp. 54-55.

6 Personal observation; Duguid op. cit., pp. 201-02.

7 The British General Staff conducted its own investigation on the question of whether the salient should be relinquished. The report recommended that the salient should be abandoned but for obvious reasons favoured the retention of Ypres.

8 'Scheme of Defence, Canadian Division,' 17 April, 1915, Appendix 330a.

9 Duguid, op. cit., vol. I, p. 222-23.

10 'Scheme of Defence, Canadian Division,' 17 April, 1915, Appendix 330a.

11 'Report on Condition of Trenches,' 21 April, 1915, Appendix 334.

12 'Scheme of Defence, Canadian Division,' 17 April, 1915, Appendix 330a.

13 General Erich von Falkenhayn, *The German General Staff and its Deci-*

sions, 1914-1916 (New York, 1920), p. 94.

14 L. Lewin, *Die Gifte in der Weltgeschichte* (Berlin, 1920); J.R. Partington, *A History of Greek Fire and Gunpowder* (Cambridge, 1960); D. Ayalon, *Gunpowder and Fire Arms in the Mamluk Kingdom* (London, 1956); W.D. Miles, 'Chapters in Chamical Warfare: I, Admiral Cochrane's Plans for Chemical Warfare; II, the Chemical Shells of Lyon Playfair,' *Armed Forces Chemical Journal*, vol. XI, 1957, pp. 22-23, 40.

15 Winston S. Churchill, *The World Crisis* (New York, 1923), vol. II, pp. 72-75.

16 Augustin M. Prentiss, *Chemicals in War* (New York, 1937), p. 132.

17 Reichsarchiv, *Der Weltkrieg, 1914-1918* (Berlin, 1932), band 8, p. 37.

18 Prentiss, op. cit., pp. 434-36.

19 Joseph Borkin, *The Crime and Punishment of I.G. Farben* (London, 1979), p. 17.

20 Gen. Max Schwarte, *Die Technik im Weltkriege* (Berlin, 1920), pp. 280-81.

21 Victor Lefebure, *The Riddle of the Rhine: Chemical Strategy in Peace and War* (New York, 1923), p. 36.

22 Prentiss, op. cit., pp. 148-51.

23 Morris Goran, *The Story of Fritz Haber* (Norman, 1967), pp. 68-69.

24 Edmonds, *France and Belgium, 1915,* vol. I, p. 188.

25 Vth Corps War Diary, 14 April, 1915, Appendix 320.

26 Général Ferry, 'Ce qui s'est passé sur l'Yser,' *La revue des vivants,* juillet 1930, pp. 899-900.

27 Edmonds, *France and Belgium, 1915,* vol. I, p. 164.

28 Vth Corps War Diary, 15 April, 1915, Appendix 323.

29 Ministère de la guerre, Etat Major de l'armée. Service Historique. *Les armées françaises dans la grande guerre,* tome II, 2e vol., annexe 1392.

30 *The Times,* 13, 14 and 19 April, 1915.

31 Vth Corps War Diary, 15 April, 1915, Appendix 320.

32 Edmonds, *France and Belgium, 1915,* vol. I, p. 165.

33 For example Currie wrote in his diary as early as 15 April that an attack was 'expected at night to be preceded by the sending of poisonous gases to our lines.' Currie diary, 15 April, 1915; MG30 E100, vol. 43, file 194, Currie papers. Similarly Victor Odlum, second in command of the 7th battalion, recalled after the war: 'We had been warned some days before that an attack would probably be made by the Germans with gas, and we were told to take necessary precautions.' Odlum in a speech given in

1923; MG30 E300, vol. 24, Odlum papers.

34 Lt. Col. William Rae to Duguid, 29 June, 1926; RG24, vol. 2680, file 2/HQC4950, Official records.

35 John Swettenham, *McNaughton* (Toronto, 1968), vol. I, p. 43.

36 C.O. of the 7th Btn.

37 Odlum in a speech given in 1923; MG30 E300, vol. 24, Odlum papers.

38 Edmonds, *France and Belgium, 1915,* vol. I, pp. 166-70.

39 Pollard, op. cit., pp. 69-76.

40 Duguid, op. cit., vol. I, p. 224; *Der Weltkrieg, 1914-1918,* band 8, pp. 38-39.

41 *Der Weltkrieg, 1914-1918,* band 8, pp. 39-40.

42 Edmonds, *France and Belgium, 1915,* vol. I, p. 189-92.

BREAK IN

1 Divisional Headquarters replied: 'There are one hundred mouth organs ... for you. Please call for them. No cards available just now but will send you some out of next consignment.' See Appendix 339.

2 German field batteries were silent from 5.00 to 5.10 PM in order not to disturb the gas clouds.

3 3rd Inf. Bde., to 1st Can. Div., Appendix 342.

4 The French Official History, which frequently places nationalism ahead of accurate reporting, is regrettably circumspect on the details following the gas attack in this sector. To learn what happened we must rely on Canadian and British sources.

5 Edmonds, *France and Belgium, 1915,* vol. I, pp. 177-78.

6 J. George Adami, *War Story of the Canadian Medical Corps* (London, 1918), pp. 103-04; Harold R. Peat, *Private Peat* (Indianapolis, 1917) pp. 143-44; Urquhart, *History of the 16th Battalion,* p. 56; Kirkpatrick diary, 22 April, 1915; MG30 E318, vol. 23, file 179, Official records.

7 Stg. Frederick Wingate's account of the gas attack, kindly made available to me by Capt. W.D. Ellis, Secretary of the Canadian Corps Cyclist Battalion Association; Victor Odlum in a speech given in 1923; MG30 E300, vol. 24, Odlum papers; and in an interview for CBC radio seris, 'Flanders' Field,' Part V, 'The Second Battle of Ypres;'F.C. Arnold and Andrew McNaughton, 7th Batt., 2nd Bde., CBC interview.

8 'Memo regarding poison gas;'RG24, vol. 1810, file GAQ1-10, Official

records.

9 Nasmith, op. cit., p. 179.

10 'Memo regarding poison gas;' RG24, vol. 1810, file GAQ1-10, Official records.

11 Andrew McNaughton, CBC interview.

12 Odlum in a speech given in 1923; MG30 E300, vol. 24, Odlum papers.

13 Elliot Green, 4th Div. Artillery, CBC interview.

14 George Patrick, 2nd Btn., ibid.

15 J. Sprostin, 9th Field Batt., ibid.

16 N. Nicholson, 16th Btn., ibid. See also H.G. Brewer, 14th Field Batt., ibid.; and Kirkpatrick diary, April 22, 1915; MG30 E318, vol. 23, file 179, Official records.

17 Maj. D.R. McCuaig, 'Report of Operations of the 13th Battalion in the Second Battale of Ypres.' This report, like some others which cannot be found in the Official archives, is appended to a work entitled *Narrative on the Formation and Operations of the First Canadian Division to the Second Battle of Ypres* (Ottawa, 1920), compiled by the Historical Section, Historical Staff.

18 Lt. Col. F.O.W. Loomis, 'Report on Action in front of Ypres, commencing 4 PM 22 April 1915' in *Operations of the First Canadian Division to the Second Battle of Ypres.*

19 The name bore no connection with Lord Kitchener but came from the French *bois des cuisiniers*.

20 3rd Inf. Bde. War Diary; MG30 E46, vol. I, file 4, Turner papers.

21 *Der Weltkrieg, 1914-1918,* band 8, pp. 40-41.

22 McCuaig report in op. cit.

23 King to Duguid, 19 May, 1926; RG24, vol. 2680, file 2/HQC4950, Official records.

24 Canadian War Records Office, *Thirty Canadian V.Cs.* (London, 1918), pp. 5-6.

25 2nd Inf. Bde. to 1st Can. Div., 22 April, 1915, Appendix 341.

26 3rd Inf. Bde. to 1st Can. Div., 22 April, 1915, Appendix 342.

27 3rd Inf. Bde. to 1st Can. Div., 22 April, 1915, Appendix 347.

28 3rd Inf. Bde. to 1st Can. Div., 22 April, 1915, Appendix 351.

29 3rd Inf. Bde. to 1st Can. Div., 22 April, 1915, Appendix 357.

30 1st Can. Div. to V Corps, 22 April, 1915, Appendix 358; to 3rd Inf. Bde., 22 April, 1915, Appendix 355; to 2nd Inf. Bde., 22 April, 1915.

31 1st Can. Div. to 16th Btn., 22 April, 1915, Appendix 353.

[32] 1st Can. Div. to 10th Btn., 22 April, 1915, Appendix 354.

[33] Currie to General MacBrien (then Chief of Staff) 24 April, 1926; RG24, vol. 2680, file 2/HQC4950, Official reocrds.

[34] V Corps to Second Army, 22 April, 1915, Appendix 374.

[35] Edmonds, *France and Belgium, 1915,* vol. I, pp. 180-81.

[36] 3rd Inf. Bde. to 1st Can. Div., April 22, 1915, Appendix 370. The message, dispatched at 8.25 PM, did not reach Divisional Headquarters until after 9 PM.

[37] Canadian survivors, interviewed for CBC, make it clear that the Germans held back on meeting the slightest resistance. Typical was the experience of Stg. Maj. C.B. Price (14th Btn.) who, along with a certain Stewart Le Mesurier, had been sent out to investigate whether the large bodies of troops ahead were French or German. Price explained: 'Just then he [Le Mesurier] saw two men coming fairly close down this hill to us and he challenged them, and one of them put up his rifle and shot him, shot him through the hand. So then just instinctively I put up my rifle and I shot both of them. And I rather think that the fact that their scouts were shot made them feel that there was a force there and instead of being able to go right through as they could have, they stopped and dug in themselves.'

[38] Adami, op. cit., Chs. V-VIII.

[39] R.G.E. Leckie, 'Account of the Charge of the 16th Battalion;' MG30 E236, vol. 4, file 7, Villiers papers.

[40] 16th Btn. War Diary; RG9, III, vol. 4925, file 396, Official records; R.G.E. Leckie, op. cit.; Lt. Col. Frank Morison, 'The 16th and 10th Canadians at St. Julien,' *Journal and Proceedings of the Hamilton Association,* vol. 30, 1918-1922, p. 142; John E. Leckie to Duguid, 28 April, 1926; RG24, vol. 2680, file 1/HQC4950, Official records.

[41] Cited in *The Times History of the War* (London, 1915), vol. V, pp. 62-63.

[42] Urquhart, *History of the 16th Battalion,* p. 59.

[43] Sir Max Aitken (later Lord Beaverbrook), *Canada in Flanders* (Toronto, 1916), vol. I, p. 56.

[44] Currie, op. cit., p. 223.

[45] R.G.E. Leckie, op. cit.

[46] D.M. Ormond, CBC interview. Ormond, then a major, took over command of the 10th Battalion after MacLaren (second in command) was struck down.

[47] Aitken, op. cit., vol. I, p. 54-55.

[48] Watson to 3rd Inf. Bde., 27 April, 1915; RG24, vol. 1822, file 5-29, Official records.

[49] 2nd Inf. Bde. to 1st Can. Div., 23 April, 1915, Appendix 412.

[50] Geddes had loaned this unit to Loomis.

[51] McCuaig report in op. cit.

[52] 1st Can. Div. to Col. Geddes, 23 April, 1915, Appendix 404.

[53] 1st Can. Div. to 1st Inf. Bde., 23 April, 1915, Appendices 399 and 408.

[54] 1st Can. Div. to 1st Inf. Bde., 23 April, 1915, Appendix 425.

[55] 1st Btn. War Diary, 23 April, 1915, Appendices A and B; RG9, III, vol. 4912, file 350, Official records; Hill to Duguid, n.d., RG24, vol. 1503, file 1/HQ683-1-30-5, Official records.

[56] Col. Hare (Can. liaison officer with the 87th French Div.) to 1st Can. Div., 23 April, 1915, Appendix 442.

[57] 1st Inf. Bde. to 1st Can. Div., 23 April, 1915, Appendices 448, 478 and 481; 1st Can. Div. to 1st Inf. Bde., 23 April, 1915, Appendices 448 and 454.

SECURING THE NEW FLANK

[1] 1st Inf. Bde. to 1st Can. Div., 23 April, 1915, Appendix 460.

[2] 1st Inf. Bde. to 1st Can. Div., 23 April, 1915, Appendices 465 and 481.

[3] McCuaig report in op. cit.

[4] Loomis to 3rd Inf. Bde., 23 April, 1915, Appendix 472.

[5] Loomis to 3rd Inf. Bde., 23 April, 1915, Appendix 461.

[6] Gordon-Hall (on Alderson's staff) to 3rd Inf. Bde., 23 April, 1915, Appendix 474.

[7] Odlum to T.G. Roberts (official report sent to Divisional Headquarters), 10 July, 1915; MG30 E300, vol. 16, Odlum papers.

[8] Odlum in a speech given in 1923; MG30 E300, vol. 24. Odlum papers.

[9] Odlum to Mrs. McHarg (Hart-McHarg's mother), 26 April, 1915; MG30 E300, vol. 16, Odlum papers.

[10] 7th Btn. War Diary, 23 April, 1915; MG30 E75, vol. 1, Urquhart papers.

[11] Odlum to T.G. Roberts, 10 July 1915; MG30 E300, vol. 16, Odlum papers.

[12] Odlum's account of Hart-McHarg's death, as told to Major Matthews,

September 1928; MG30 E300, vol. 16, Odlum papers.

13 Odlum in a speech given in 1923; MG30 E300, vol. 24, Odlum papers.

14 Odlum to Currie, date unknown; MG30 E300, vol. 16, Odlum papers.

15 Odlum's account of Hart-McHarg's death, as told to Major Matthews, September 1928; MG30 E300, vol. 16, Odlum papers.

16 Ibid.

17 Sir George Arthur, *Life of Lord Kitchener* (London, 1920), vol. III, p. 233.

18 *Les armées françaises dans la grande guerre,* tome II, p. 701.

19 On this subject see especially Capt. B.H. Liddell Hart, *Foch: The Man of Orleans* (Boston, 1932) and Gen. Sir James Marshall-Cornwall, *Foch as Military Commander* (New York, 1972).

20 *Der Weltkrieg, 1914-1918,* band 8, pp. 41-43.

21 Quiquandon to 1st Can. Div., 23 April, 1915, Appendix 485.

22 1st Can. Div. to 13th Inf. Bde.; to Geddes' Detachment; to 1st and 3rd Inf. Bdes., 23 April, 1915, Appendix 486.

23 13th Inf. Bde. to 1st Can. Div., 23 April, 1915, Appendix 497.

24 G.W. Twigg, 4th Btn., CBC interview.

25 Edmonds, *France and Belgium, 1915,* vol. I, p. 207.

26 Duguid, op. cit., vol. I, p. 283-84.

27 Gordon-Hall to Duguid, 27 April, 1926; RG24, vol. 2680, file 2/HQC4950, Official records.

28 Loomis report in op. cit.

29 McCuaig report in op. cit.

30 *Les armées françaises dans la grande guerre,* tome II, p. 703.

31 Edmonds, *France and Belgium, 1915,* vol. I, Appendix 22.

THE DAY OF CRISIS

1 *Der Weltkrieg, 1914-1918,* band 8, pp. 42-44.

2 *Les armées françaises dans la grande guerre,* tome II, p. 706.

3 3rd Art. Bde. to 3rd Inf. Bde., 24 April, 1915, Appendix 526.

4 The British Command had requested respirators from home but until these arrived it was left to the divisions to make for themselves. The requisite muslin, flannel, gauze and elastic could not be obtained locally in large quantities and that explains why only a few units were equipped

with improvised gas masks on the morning of 24 April.

5 Nasmith, op. cit., p. 186.

6 15th Btn. War Diary, 24 April, 1915, in *Operations of the First Canadian Division to the Second Battle of Ypres;* 8th Btn. War Diary, 24 April, 1915; RG9, III, vol. 4870, file 201/15-4, Official records; Kim Beattie, *The 48th Highlanders of Canada* (Toronto, 1932), pp. 70-71.

7 Lt. Col. H.H. Matthews, 'An Account of the Second Battle of Ypres, April 1915;' MG30 E60, vol. 4, file 17, Matthews papers. The author was in command of No. 2 Company, 8th Can. Btn., and this story was written for friends in June 1915, a few weeks after the fighting ended.

8 J. Upritchard, 8th Btn., CBC interview.

9 Tuxford to Duguid, 15 April, 1926; RG24, vol. 2680, file 1/HQC4950, Official records.

10 Report of No. 3 Company, 15th Btn., 24 April, 1915, MG30 E46, vol. 1, file 4, Turner papers; 15th Btn. War Diary, 24 April, 1915 in op. cit.

11 3rd Inf. Bde. to 2nd Inf. Bde.; to 1st Can. Div., 24 April, 1915, Appendices 528 and 529.

12 *Thirty Canadian V.Cs.,* pp. 7-9.

13 McCuaig report in op. cit.

14 15th Btn. War Diary, 24 April, 1915, in op. cit.; Beattie, op. cit., pp. 74-75.

15 3rd Inf. Bde. to 1st Can. Div., 24 April, 1915, Appendix 529.

16 2nd Inf. Bde. to 1st Can. Div., 24 April, 1915, Appendix 536.

17 3rd Inf. Bde. to 1st Can. Div., 24 April, 1915, Appendix 539.

18 3rd Inf. Bde. to 1st Can. Div., 24 April, 1915, Appendix 542.

19 1st Can. Div. to York and Durham (150th Bde.), 24 April, 1915, Appendix 544.

20 1st Can. Div. to York and Durham, 24 April, 1915, Appendix 549.

21 1st Can. Div. to 3rd Inf. Bde., 24 April, 1915, Appendix 557.

22 7th Btn. War Diary, 24 April, 1915; MG30 E75, vol. 1, Urquhart papers.

23 The *London Gazette,* 13 May, 1919; Odlum to Currie, date undecipherable; MG30 E300, vol. 16, Odlum papers.

24 He was the acting commander. The commanding officer, Lt. Col. F.S. Meighen, had been placed in charge of the troops in the GHQ Line.

25 An area that cannot be reached by enemy fire.

26 Beattie, op. cit., pp. 76-77; Loomis report in op. cit.

27 Watson to Turner, 27 April, 1915; RG24, vol. 1822, file 5-29,

Official records; Col. W.W. Murray, *The History of the 2nd Canadian Battalion in the Great War, 1914-1919* (Ottawa, 1947), p. 51.

28 1st Can. Div. to 3rd Inf. Bde., 24 April, 1915, Appendix 566.

29 1st Can. Div. to 3rd Inf. Bde., 24 April, 1915, Appendix 580; 1st Can. Div. War Diary, 24 April, 1915; RG9, III, vol. 4823, Official records.

30 3rd Inf. Bde. to 5th Durhams; to 4th Yorks; to 2nd, 3rd, 13th, 14th, 15th and 16th Btns., 24 April, 1915, Appendix 586.

31 Duguid, op. cit., vol. I, p. 311.

32 In a personal note to the Canadian Chief of Staff, dated 23 June, 1936, Duguid writes: "The fact is that, in my story, the truth and nothing but the truth has been told, but out of consideration for General Turner not the whole truth: his actions and their results are made clear without comment and without stressing what Gordon-Hall describes as 'their disastrous consequences.'"; RG24, vol. 2680, file 2/HQC4950, Official records.

33 Gordon-Hall to Duguid, 16 January, 1935; RG24, vol, 1503, file 1/HQ683-1-30-5, Official records.

34 Several months later Alderson attempted in vain to prevent Turner's appointment as commander of the newly formed 2nd Canadian Division. He wrote the following: 'I am sorry to say that I do not consider Turner really fit to command a Division and his name was not put forward for it by Sir John French, but Canadian politics have been too strong for all of us and so he has got it.' Alderson to Hutton, 21 August, 1915; Add. MS. 50096, p. 310, Hutton papers (British Musueum, London). I am indebted to Professor Desmond Morton for sending my a copy of the letter.

35 Sutherland Brown to J.A. MacBrien (Canadian Chief of Staff), 25 November, 1925; RG24, vol. 2680, file 1/HQC4950, Official records.

36 Ibid.

37 George Patrick, 2nd Btn., CBC interview.

38 Murray, op. cit., pp. 53-54; Report of No. 2 Co., 2nd Btn., April 24, 1915; MG30 E318, vol. 23, file 178B, Official records.

39 E. Seamen, 3rd Btn., CBC interview.

40 Maj. Kirkpatrick diary, 24 April, 1915; MG30 E318, vol. 23, file 179, Official records.

41 G.O.C. 27th Div. to 3rd Inf. Bde., 24 April, 1915, Appendix 600.

42 3rd Inf. Bde. to G.O.C. 27th Div., 24 April, 1915, Appendix 631.

43 Urquhart, *Arthur Currie,* pp. 75-87; 8th Btn. War Diary, 24 April,

1915; RG9, III, vol. 4870, file 201/15-4, Official records.

44 Currie to Duguid, 15 April, 1926; MG30 E100, vol. 8, file 22, Currie papers.

45 Currie's biographer.

46 Urquhart to Duguid, 5 December, 1934; RG24, vol. 1503, file 1/HQ683-1-30-5, Official records.

47 Currie to Duguid, 15 April, 1926; MG30 E100, vol. 8, file 22, Currie papers.

48 Ibid.

49 Edmonds to Duguid, 23 September and 12 November, 1936; RG24, vol. 1503, file 3/HQ683-1-30-5, Official records.

50 Lynn to Urquhart, 22 June, 1936; MG30 E75, vol. 2, file 3, Urquhart papers. Lynn kept a copious record of everything that concerned or interested him since the day he enlisted with the 2nd Btn., R.G.R.I. on October 21, 1899, while he was only seventeen. This lengthy and graphic account of the Snow-Currie interview, from which I obtained most of my information, was based on his diary.

51 Ibid.

52 Currie to Duguid, 15 April 1926; MG30 E100, vol. 8, file 22, Currie papers.

53 Lynn to Urquhart, 22 June, 1936; MG30 E75, vol. 2, file 3, Urquhart papers.

54 Ibid.

55 Currie to Duguid, 15 April 1926; MG30 E100, vol. 8, file 22, Currie papers.

56 1st Can. Div. to 3rd Inf. Bde., 24 April, 1915, Appendix 612.

57 *Les armées françaises dans la grande guerre,* tome II, p. 706.

58 Edmonds, *France and Belgium, 1915,* vol. I, Appendix 23.

59 Foch to French, 24 April, 1915, Appendix 613.

60 The 2nd King's Own Yorkshire Light Infantry and the 9th London (13th Bde.); the 4th Canadian; the 1st Royal Irish Regiment (27th Div.); and the 12th London and 1st Suffolk (28th Div.).

61 V Corps to 1st Can. Div., 24 April, 1915, Appendix 619.

62 Lt. Gen. Alderson, 'Operation Order No. 10,' 24 April, 1915, Appendix 627.

63 The forces under Turner's command consisted of the remains of the 2nd, 3rd, 14th and 16th Canadians, the two York and Durham battalions, the 2nd East Kent and one and a half companies of the 9th London.

[64] 3rd Inf. Bde. to 1st Can. Div., 24 April, 1915, Appendix 630.

[65] 3rd Inf. Bde. to G.O.C. 27th Div., 24 April, 1915, Appendices 618 and 631.

[66] V Corps to 1st Can. Div., 24 April 1915, Appendix 634.

RELIEF AT LAST

[1] 1st Can. Div. to 10th Inf. Bde., 25 April, 1915, Appendix 640.

[2] Duguid, op. cit., vol. I, p. 347.

[3] Edmonds, *France and Belgium, 1915,* vol. I, pp. 240-43.

[4] *Der Weltkrieg, 1914-1918,* band 8, pp. 44-45.

[5] *France and Belgium, 1915,* vol. I, pp. 245-46.

[6] 8th Btn. War Diary, 25 April, 1915; RG9, III, vol. 4870, file 201/15-4, Official records; Matthews, op. cit.; MG30 E60, vol. 4, file 17, Matthews papers.

[7] 8th Btn. War Diary, 25 April, 1915; RG9, III, vol. 4870, file 201/15-4, Official records; 2nd Inf. Bde. War Diary, 25 April, 1915; MG30 E60, vol. 4, Matthews papers.

[8] W. Critchley, 10th Btn., CBC interview.

[9] 8th Btn. War Diary, 25 April, 1915; RG9, III, vol. 4870, file 201/15-4, Official records; Matthews, op. cit.; MG30 E60, vol. 4, file 17, Matthews papers.

[10] 1st Can Div. to 2nd Inf. Bde., 25 April, 1915, Appendix 659.

[11] 1st Can. Div. to 10th Inf. Bde., 25 April, 1915, Appendix 664.

[12] 5th Div. to 1st Can. Div., 25 April, 1915; 1st Can. Div. to 10th Inf. Bde.; to 2nd Bde. HQ Wieltje, 25 April, 1915, Appendices 665 and 666; Duguid, op. cit., vol. I, pp. 354-55.

[13] F.C. Bagshaw, 5th Btn. CBC interview.

[14] 2nd Inf. Bde. War Diary, 25 April, 1915; MG30 E60, vol. 4, Matthews papers.

[15] 7th Btn. War Diar, 25 April, 1915; MG30 E75, vol. 1, Urquhart papers; Odlum, CBC interview.

[16] 2nd Inf. Bde. War Diary, 25 April, 1915; MG30 E60, vol. 4, Matthews papers.

[17] Ibid.

[18] Steevens to 2nd Inf. Bde., 25 April, 1915, Appendix 672.

[19] 2nd Inf. Bde. War Diary, 25 April, 1915; MG30 E60, vol. 4, Matthews papers.

[20] Cited in CBC radio program.

[21] 8th Btn. War Diary, 25 April, 1915; RG9, III, vol. 4870, file 201/15-4, Official records.

[22] A.H. Fisher, 8th Btn., CBC interview.

[23] 5th Btn. War Diary, 25 April, 1915; MG30 E239, Hilliam papers.

[24] 2nd Inf. Bde. War Diary, 25 April, 1915; MG30 E60, vol. 4, Matthews papers.

[25] 7th Btn. War Diary, 25 April, 1915; MG30 E75, vol. 1, Urquhart papers;

[26] *Thirty Canadian V.Cs.*, pp. 9-10; Adami, op. cit., pp. 146-47; *Canadian Gazette,* 22 July, 1915.

[27] Edmonds, *France and Belgium, 1915,* vol. I, Appendix 25.

[28] Gen Alderson, 'Operation Order No. 11,' 25 April, 1915, Appendix 675.

[29] *Les armées françaises dans la grande guerre,* tome II, p. 708.

[30] Edmonds, *France and Belgium, 1915,* vol. I, pp. 256-63.

[31] *Les armées françaises dans la grande guerre,* tome II, pp. 709-10.

[32] Ibid., tome II, 2e vol., annexe 1461.

[33] Ibid., tome II, 2e vol., annexe. 1460.

[34] Edmonds, *France and Belgium, 1915,* vol. I, Appendix 29.

[35] Ibid., Appendix 30.

[36] For details of the incident see A.J. Smithers, *The Man Who Disobeyed* (London, 1970), Ch. XXI; Brig.-Gen. C. Ballard, *Smith-Dorrien* (London, 1931), Ch. XVIII; and Cassar, op. cit., pp. 224-5.

[37] *Les armées françaises dans la grande guerre,* tome II, 2e vol., annexe 1466.

[38] Ibid., annexe 1468.

[39] 1st Can. Div. to 1st Inf. Bde.; to 3rd Inf. Bde.; to 13th Bde., 28 April, 1915, Appendix 694.

[40] Murray, op. cit., pp. 59-60.

[41] Gen. Alderson, 'Operation Order No. 13,' 2 May, 1915, Appendix 699.

EPILOGUE

[1] R.H. Williams, op. cit., vol. I, Ch. II

[2] Jeffrey Williams, op. cit., p. 12.

[3] *Der Weltkrieg, 1914-1918,* band 8, pp. 47-48.

[4] Edmonds, *France and Belgium, 1915,* vol. I, pp. 304-6.

5 R.H. Williams, op. cit., vol. I, pp. 60-64.

6 H.W. Niven, P.P.C.L.I., CBC interview.

7 Cited in Duguid, op. cit., vol. I, p. 405.

8 Gordon-Hall to Duguid, 16 January, 1935; RG24, vol. 1503, file 1/HQ683-1-30-5, Official records.

9 French to the War Office, 15 June, 1915, Appendix 705.

10 'Alderson's Speech to the 1st Canadian Division,' 4 May, 1915; MG30 E92, Alderson papers.

11 Duguid, op. cit., vol. I, p. 421.

12 Andrew McNaughton on the origins of 'In Flanders Fields,' MG30 E133, vol. 4, McNaughton papers.

BIBLIOGRAPHY

I. MANUSCRIPT COLLECTIONS

The following sets of unpublished papers used in the preparation of this work, unless otherwise stated, are housed at the Public Archives in Ottawa.

Alderson papers. These consist only of a thin file.

Robert Borden papers.

J.J. Creelman papers. CO, 2nd Brigade, Canadian Field Artillery.

Arthur Currie papers.

Sir John French papers. Imperial War Museum, London.

Edward Hilliam papers. Adjutant of the 5th Battalion.

Henry Lamb papers.

John Edward Leckie papers. Served as a major in the 16th Battalion (Canadian Scottish) along with his older brother Robert who was the CO.

Robert Gilmore Leckie papers.

Andrew McNaughton papers. Canadian Field Artillery.

Harold Halford Matthews papers. Company CO, 8th Battalion.

Victor Odlum papers.

Official records. These include the massive Duguid correspondence and various unit papers, as well as the War Diaries of the Division, the Brigades and the Battalions.

George Perley papers

Horace Smith-Dorrien papers. Imperial War Museum, London.

Richard Turner papers.

Hugh Urquhart papers. Currie's biographer served in the 16th Battalion and later became its historian.

Paul F. Villiers papers. 3rd Canadian Brigade staff.

II. OFFICIAL AND REGIMENTAL HISTORIES

Aiken, Max (later Lord Beaverbrook). *Canada in Flanders,* vol. I. Toronto, 1916.

Beattie, Kim. *48th Highlanders of Canada, 1891-1928,* vol. I.

Toronto, 1932.

Duguid, Colonel A. Fortescue. *Official History of the Canadian Forces in the Great War, 1914-1919,* vol. I. Ottawa, 1938. After peace had been restored Colonel Duguid, the Director of the Historical Section, was instructed to compile an eight-volume official history of the Canadian Army in the Great War. The first was published in 1938, together with a volume of appendices and maps. It covered the period from August 1914 to September 1915. The outbreak of the Second World War, however, followed by the retirement of Duguid, led the authorities to cancel the project.

Edmonds, Brig.-Gen. Sir James E. *Official History of the Great War. Military Operations. France and Belgium, 1915,* vol. I. London, 1927. An uninformed person, reading Edmonds' account of 'Second Ypres,' would get a somewhat distorted picture of what really occurred during the critical days of the battle. Whether he was conscious of it or not, the author clearly underplayed the extent and significance of the Canadian contribution. But long before the relevant material went into print some Canadians, Duguid in particular, did their best to set the record straight.

In 1925 several senior Canadian officers, invited to comment on the first draft of the three chapters dealing with Second Ypres in the British Official History, were appalled by the implication that General Snow, with the assistance of Wanless O'Gowan and Major Moulton-Barrett of the Northumberland Fusiliers, had saved the day. Duguid wrote a 53 page critique, expressing Canadian concerns and correcting the many factual errors. Edmonds was unruffled by the uproar which his preliminary draft had created in Canadian military circles. He replied that the Canadian Division would receive the same consideration as any other British unit and that, if any discrepancies between accounts proved irreconcilable, they would be treated in the footnotes with both versions given.

In the second draft Edmonds failed to respond to the substance of Duguid's criticism and made only minor changes. This version, read by more than two dozen senior officers who had served in the 1st Division, both British and Canadians, received a reception no less hostile than the original one. All these officers were struck by the anti-Canadian bias which permeated the narrative. Edmonds, Currie wrote, 'appears to be determined that, so far as it lies within his power to influence their judgment and imagination, future generations must not be allowed to think that Dominion troops were comparable in any degree with their brothers-in-arms recruited in the Old Country.'

The Chief of the Canadian General Staff was sufficiently aroused to warn his British counterpart that, unless the Canadian effort at Ypres was treated with more objectivity in the Official History, he would encourage his government to lodge an official protest with the Secretary of State for Dominion Affairs in London. Under pressure from his own military superiors Edmonds did make modest changes in the final draft but he refused to send it to Ottawa as had been requested.

Fetherstonhaugh, R.C. *The Royal Montreal Regiment, 14th Battalion, CEF, 1914-1925*. Montreal, 1927.

——. *The 13th Battalion Royal Highlanders of Canada, 1914-1919*. Montreal 1925.

France, Ministère de la guerre, Etat Major de l'armée. Service Historique. *Les armées françaises dans la grande guerre,* tome II and accompanying volume of annexes. Paris, 1930.

Macphail, Andrew. *Official History of the Canadian Forces in the Great War, 1914-1919: The Medical Services*. Ottawa, 1925.

Murray, W.W. *The History of the 2nd Canadian Battalion in the Great War, 1914-1919*. Ottawa, 1947.

Nicholson, Colonel G.W.L. *Official History of the Canadian Army in the First World War: Canadian Expeditionary Force, 1914-1919*. Ottawa, 1962. In 1956 the Canadian Government, in response to requests from individuals and veterans' organizations, authorized Colonel Nicholson, then Deputy Director of the Historical Section, to write a one volume study of the achievements of the Canadian Expeditionary Force in the Great War. Overall Nicholson produced an admirable account but his treatment of the first year of the war is essentially a condensation of Duguid's volume. He appears to have paid scant attention to the enormous collection of documents and records on the period that were assembled by Duguid and his staff.

Reichsarchiv. *Der Weltkrieg, 1914-1918,* band 8, Berlin, 1932.

Scudmore, T.V. *A Short History of the 7th Battalion, CEF,* Vancouver, 1930.

Urquhart, H.M. *The History of the 16th Battalion (the Canadian Scottish) in the Great War, 1914-1919.* Toronto, 1932.

Williams, Jeffrey. *Princess Patricia's Canadian Light Infantry.* London, 1972.

Williams, Ralph Hodder. *Princess Patricia's Canadian Light Infantry, 1914-1919,* vol. I. Toronto, 1923.

III. PRIMARY AND SECONDARY SOURCES

Adami, J.G. *War Story of the Canadian Army Medical Corps,* vol. I. London, 1918.

Anonymous. *Unknown Soldier by One of Them.* New York, 1959.

Armstrong, Elizabeth H. *The Crisis of Quebec.* New York, 1937.

Arthur, Sir George. *Life of Lord Kitchener,* vol. III. London, 1920.

Ayalon, D. *Gunpowder and Fire Arms in the Mamluk Kingdom.* London, 1956.

Ballard, Brig.-Gen. C. *Smith-Dorrien.* London, 1931.

Baeur, Max. *Der Grosse Krieg im Feld und Heimat.* Tübingen, 1921.

Bidwell, Shelford, and Graham, Dominick. *Fire-Power: British Army Weapons and Theories of War 1904-1945.* London, 1982.

Borden, Robert Laird. *His Memoirs,* vol. I. New York, 1938.

Borkin, Joseph. *The Crime and Punishment of I.G. Farben.* London, 1978.

Canada, House of Commons, *Debates.*

Canadian War Records Office. *Thirty Canadian VCs.* London, 1918.

Cassar, George H. *The Tragedy of Sir John French.* Cranbury, 1985.

CBC transcript of radio series 'Flanders' Fields,' Part 5, 'The Second Battle of Ypres.' A copy can be obtained from the CBC Library in Toronto.

Churchill, Winston S. *The World Crisis,* vol. II. New York, 1951.

Currie, Colonel J.A. *The Red Watch: With the First Canadian Division in Flanders.* Toronto, 1916.

Giles, John. *The Ypres Salient.* London, 1970.

Goran, Morris, *The Story of Fritz Haber.* Norman, 1967.

Harrington, General Sir Charles. *Plumer of Messines*. London, 1935.

Historical Section, General Staff. *The Western Front, 1914*. Ottawa, 1957.

Historical Section, Historical Staff. *Narrative on the Formation and Operation of the First Canadian Division to the Second Battle of Ypres* (Ottawa, 1920). This account is most unreliable and should not be used as a work of reference. The work as a whole is valuable, however, because it contains the battalion War Diaries, several of which cannot be found in the Official records. A copy of the publication, which had a very limited circulation, can be found at the National Defence Headquarters Library in Ottawa.

Hyatt, A.M.J. 'The Military Career of Sir Arthur Currie.' Duke University Ph.D. thesis, 1965.

Johnson, Douglas Wilson. *Battlefields of the World War*. New York, 1921.

Lefebure, Victor. *The Riddle of the Rhine: Chemical Strategy in Peace and War*. New York, 1923.

Lewin, L. *Die Gifte in der Weltgeschichte*. Berlin, 1920.

Liddell Hart, Captain B.H. *Foch: The Man of Orleans*. Boston, 1932.

Lucas, Sir Charles. *The Empire at War*, vol. II. London, 1923.

Marshall-Cornwall, General Sir James. *Foch as Military Commander*. New York, 1972.

——. *Haig as Military Commander*. New York, 1973.

Nasmith, Colonel George G. *Canada's Sons and Great Britian in the World War*. Toronto, 1919.

Partington, J.R. *A History of Greek Fire and Gunpowder*. Cambridge, 1960.

Peat, Harold R. *Private Peat*. Indianapolis, 1917.

Pollard, Hugh B.C. *The Story of Ypres*. New York, 1917.

Prentiss, Augustin M. *Chemicals in War*. New York, 1937.

Schwarte, General Max. *Die Technik im Weltkriege*. Berlin, 1920.

Skelton, Oscar Douglas. *Life and Letters of Sir Wilfred Laurier*, vol. II. New York, 1922.

Smithers, A.J. *The Man Who Disobeyed*. London, 1970.

Stanley, G.F.G. *Canada's Soldiers, 1604-1954*. Toronto, 1954.

Swettenham, John. *McNaughton*, vol. I. Toronto, 1968.

——. *To Seize the Victory*. Toronto, 1965.

The Times History of the War, vol. V. London, 1915.

Tuchman, Barbara. *The Guns of August.* New York, 1962.

Urquhart, Hugh M. *Arthur Currie: The Biography of a Great Canadian,* Toronto, 1950.

Various authorities. *Canada in the Great World War,* vol. III. Toronto, 1919.

Von Falkenhayn, General Erich. *The German General Staff and its Decisions, 1914-1916.* New York, 1920.

Winter, Brig.-Gen. Charles F. *The Hon. Sir Sam Hughes.* Toronto, 1931.

IV. ARTICLES

Ferry, General. 'Ce qui s'est passé sur l'Yser,' *La revue des vivants,* juillet, 1930.

Graham, Dominick. '*Sans Doctrine:* British Army Tactics in the First World War' in Timothy Travers and Christon Archer, eds., *Men at War.* Chicago, 1982.

Haber, Fritz. 'Chemistry in War,' *Journal of Chemical Education,* November, 1945.

Impressions of a Platoon Commander. 'The Canadian Scottish at the Second Battle of Ypres, April 1915,' *Canadian Defence Quarterly,* vol. II, 1924-25.

Miles, W.D., 'Chapters in Chemical Warfare: I, Admiral Cochrane's plans for Chemical Warfare; II, The Chemical Shells of Lyon Playfair,' *Armed Forces Chemical Journal,* vol. II, 1957.

Morison, Lt.-Col. Frank. 'The 16th and 10th Canadians at St. Julien,' *Journal and Proceedings of the Hamilton Association,* vol. XXX, 1918-22.

Morton, Desmond. 'Exerting Control: The Development of Canadian Authority Over the Canadian Expeditionary Force, 1914-1919,' in Timothy Travers and Christon Archer, eds., *Men at War.* Chicago, 1982.

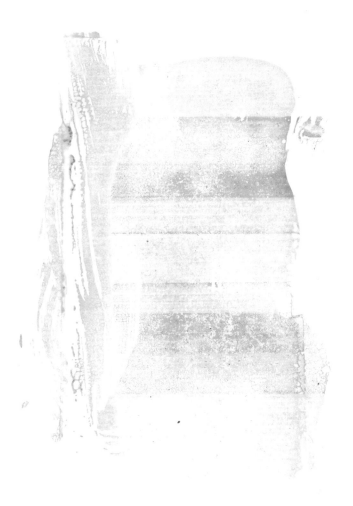